Strategic Intervention Practice Book

Grade 5

Harcourt School Publishers

www.harcourtschool.com

Printed in the United States of America

ISBN 10: 0-15-365533-X
ISBN 13: 978-0-15-365533-3

6 7 8 9 10 073 17 16 14 13 12 11 10 09

humiliation	for	bandage
expectations	her	chest
fringes	looked	dusk
hesitating	so	does
sincere	there	switch
coaxed	to	timid
	were	trust

1. We had to put / a bandage / on the dog's chest.

2. I felt humiliation / for the people / who would not help / this dog.

3. My expectations / for the dog's behavior / were exceeded.

4. We took the dogs / to the fringes of town, / so they could run around.

5. Does the veterinarian / need to be coaxed / into letting the dog / go home?

6. The dog's owner / is so sincere / that it's impossible / not to trust her.

7. I already fed the dog twice, / so I was hesitating / before I fed her again.

8. I swept the floor / to pick up all / of the dog's hair.

9. There were people / walking their dogs / at dusk.

10. The timid dog / looked for his bone.

"No Expectations" • Practice Book
© Harcourt • Grade 5

Name _____

Read the sentences. Write S if it is a complete sentence and write F if it is a fragment.

1. Mike, Sam, and I. _____

2. The dog loves to sleep by the fireplace. _____

3. Ran down the street! _____

4. Do you like to walk dogs? _____

5. Said he would help. _____

Read the sentences. Write D if it is a declarative sentence and write I if it is an interrogative sentence.

6. Charlie fed the dog four times today. _____

7. Did your dog get its shots yet? _____

8. Does your dog know how to obey commands? _____

9. I love taking Sam on hikes. _____

10. I bought my dog a new leash. _____

"No Expectations" • Practice Book
© Harcourt • Grade 5

It is important for a writer to express a personal **voice**, or personality, to make his or her writing unique.

The author's personality is revealed. → Voice ← Voice can be expressed through honesty and humor.

A. Read the passage. Look for details that reveal what the writer thinks and feels.

My little sister, Sarah, was just born last week. Sarah has chubby cheeks and bright pink lips. Her eyes are blue, and she has curly black hair. Sarah is so precious and hardly ever cries. Holding Sarah makes me feel incredible. I am going to be a good big sister to Sarah. But I'm glad it's not me that has to get up in the night when she cries!

B. Find words in the passage to complete each direction.

1. Circle the descriptive words that describe the way Sarah looks.

2. Underline the words that show the writer's positive viewpoint.

3. Draw a box around the sentence that shows honesty or humor.

C. On a separate sheet of paper, write a short character description that reveals your personality and thoughts about someone. Use honesty and humor to relay your feelings. Remember to use descriptive words!

"No Expectations" • Practice Book
© Harcourt • Grade 5

Read the story. Then circle the letter of the answer that makes each sentence below tell about the story.

Getting my first pet was one of the most exciting things that has ever happened to me. I never thought this day would come. I felt both excited and nervous when I heard my mom ask, "Are you ready to go?" I wondered, "Would I know how to take care of it? What if it does not want to leave the pet store?" These ideas raced through my mind.

When we finally got to the shelter, I ran right to the kittens. I knew which one I wanted right away. We picked up the other stuff we would need—food, a collar, toys—while we were there.

When we got home, the kitten seemed timid. My mom said it would probably just take her a while to come out of her shell. I said, "Mom, she's not a turtle!" My mom laughed and told me that was just an expression that means she would become more comfortable. I decided to name her Stretch. I placed Stretch on a plaid pillow to sleep. I am very fond of my new kitten, and I think we will be good friends.

1. What is a question that the author has?
   A "What if I can't afford it?"
   B "What if I can't take care of it?"
   C "What if it does not want to leave the pet store?"
   D "What if I can't find one I like?"

2. What supplies do they buy at the shelter?
   A food and a leash
   B food, a collar, and toys
   C a collar, food, and food dishes
   D a bed, food, and toys

3. Which word describes how the cat behaved when they first brought her home?
   A timid
   B hyper
   C sad
   D rowdy

4. What name was given to the kitten?
   A Mitch
   B Spot
   C Fetch
   D Stretch

5. Where did the author place the kitten to sleep?
   A on a plaid pillow
   B on a striped pillow
   C in a bed
   D on the couch

6. The author is fond of the kitten. What does *fond* mean?
   A timid or scared
   B trusting
   C having love or affection
   D lonely

maven	her	twice
mortified	sometimes	obtain
reigned	was	eager
conceited	she	saying
designated	said	coach
smirk	the	smoke
exhilarated	to	

1. Cathy Freeman / was a track maven / because she worked hard.

2. Cathy was eager / to follow / her dreams.

3. When Cathy won, / she made sure / not to act conceited.

4. Cathy reigned / as "The Queen / of Track."

5. New Zealand / was the designated location / for the contest.

6. Someone heard / Cathy's coach / saying to her, / "Don't ever / be mortified."

7. Cathy would smile, / and not smirk, / at the end / of each race.

8. Sometimes, / Cathy would sleep late / to obtain / the most rest she could.

9. Cathy ran / the track twice / and felt exhilarated.

10. Cathy didn't smoke / because she wanted / to stay healthy.

Read the sentences below. Tell if the sentence is *imperative*, *exclamatory*, or *both*. Then add the correct punctuation at the end of the sentence.

1. That is such a fast car _____

2. Raise your hand to ask a question _____

3. Always treat other people with respect _____

4. Never do that again _____

5. What a nice dog _____

6. Please be careful _____

Add the correct punctuation to the interjection in each sentence.

7. Quiet the baby is sleeping _____

8. Help _____

9. Wow you ate the whole pizza _____

10. Stop _____

11. Gosh that's an amazing story _____

12. Hey I just finished that _____

Name _____

In an autobiography, **voice** refers to the fact that a writer's personality can be revealed through the tone of his or her writing.

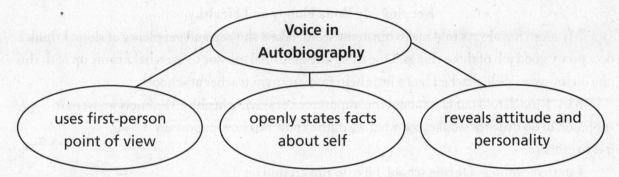

A. Read the story below. Then fill in the chart.

I like to run track. I find it relieves stress. I often run with my friends after school. We have races to challenge each other. I usually win the races, because I can run very fast. I have long legs that help me run. I always wear comfortable running shoes so that I don't get blisters. Even when I feel tired, I never quit. I know what it takes to become a winner.

Autobiographical Character Description		
Appearance	Abilities	Relationships

B. Read the paragraph below. Draw a line under words that describe *appearance*, draw two lines under words that describe *abilities*, and circle words that tell about *relationships*.

I was Cathy's track coach. I am a track maven. I was excited to teach Cathy about track. I love running, just as much as she does. I can run very fast. Sometimes I run barefoot, but mostly I use sturdy shoes and wear cool clothing. Cathy and I developed a close relationship. We like to run together.

C. On a separate sheet of paper, write a short paragraph about yourself. Include ideas about appearance, abilities, and relationships.

"Cathy Freeman" • **Practice Book**
© Harcourt • Grade 5

Decoding/Spelling:
Words with Long
Vowels and Vowel
Digraphs
. . . .
Lesson 2

Name _____

Read the story. Circle the words with long vowel sounds or vowel digraphs.

Keeping My Body Happy and Healthy

My mom has always told me to brush my teeth, take a shower, and get plenty of sleep. I think I do a pretty good job of those things. One thing she didn't tell me was to exercise. I came up with this one on my own. Well, maybe I had a little help from my gym teacher at school.

Mrs. Kindell told our class about the importance of staying healthy. We knew we weren't supposed to do drugs or smoke, but what we didn't know was how important it is to exercise.

I started running. During school, I like to run around on the playground. After school, I run on the track team I joined. I really love running, and now I run twice as fast!

Circle and write the word with a long vowel sound that best completes each sentence.

1. It is important to get plenty of _____ at night.

   sleep   eat   meat

2. I don't want cavities, so I make sure to brush my _____.

   needle   teeth   knees

3. My _____ taught me that exercise is important.

   human   teacher   niece

4. It isn't healthy to do drugs or _____.

   smoke   faint   sleep

5. I joined the track _____.

   speech   team   saying

6. Now I run _____ as fast.

   eager   reason   twice

"Cathy Freeman" • Practice Book

Name _____

pried	was	counter
desperately	could	fraud
sneered	he	awning
indignantly	said	laundry
urgently	she	feud
grudgingly	the	annoying
	they	rescue

1. Walt desperately wanted / to help out / his family.

2. The boy / did not offer grudgingly, / as he was glad / to help.

3. When the hurricane came, / the residents / reacted urgently.

4. Tim and his dad / did not think / it was annoying / to come / to the rescue.

5. The two boys / could have sneered at each other / and had a feud, / but instead / they worked together.

6. Walt knew / if he said something indignantly, / his mom / would be upset.

7. The wind was so strong / it caused an awning / to fall and hit / the kitchen counter.

8. The wind whipped the laundry / from the clothesline / and pried up the pole.

9. The police were glad / when they found out / that fraud was not involved.

10. The heavy wind / from the storm / blew branches / to the ground.

"Walt Helps Out" • Practice Book
© Harcourt • Grade 5

Name _____

Read the sentences below. Circle the subject. Underline the predicate. If a sentence is a fragment, rewrite it as a complete sentence on a separate sheet of paper.

1. The wind blew leaves off the trees.

2. All of the children.

3. The baker made bread every week.

4. The river was flooding the city.

5. The new restaurant in town.

6. Scored many points in last week's game.

7. Firefighters serve their community.

8. The girls are going shopping.

9. Last week's math test was very difficult.

10. Are a good source of vitamins.

"Walt Helps Out" • Practice Book
© Harcourt • Grade 5

Name _____

Word choice can make your writing more effective. Good
writers choose their words carefully in order to convey ideas
precisely and create a clear picture in the reader's mind. Good writers use vivid words
when describing people, places, things, or events to make their ideas come to life.

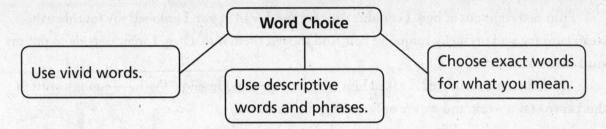

Word Choice

Use vivid words.

Use descriptive
words and phrases.

Choose exact words
for what you mean.

A. Read the story below. Underline vivid and descriptive words.

Example   The tranquil wind made the leaves rustle.

It was a beautiful summer day. As I walked through the park, I observed
the deep green leaves on the trees. The sun was piercing hot though, so I
decided to sit down and unwind. When I sat on the grass, I noticed it was
dry and brittle, as there had not been precipitation in quite some time.

I was parched. I took a sip from my bottle of water to quench my thirst. Suddenly, I heard a
noise coming from behind me. I peered around the tree to see what it was. A dog was lying there,
panting heavily. I decided to share my water. As he eagerly lapped it up from my hand, I knew he
was delighted that I shared!

B. Read the paragraph below. Underline vivid verbs and circle precise adjectives.

Example   The (immense) train jolted on the tracks.

The enormous airplane glided through the sky. The piercing roar could be heard from
the crowd on the ground. The numerous fans applauded the pilot. As the plane landed, the
adventurous pilot grinned as the fans warmly greeted him.

**C. On a separate sheet of paper, write a short paragraph to model word choice. Use
the previous passages as examples.**

"Walt Helps Out" • Practice Book
© Harcourt • Grade 5

Name _____

Read the story. Circle the words with the variant vowel sounds /ow/, /oi/, /ô/, /o͞o/, and /yo͞o/.

Decoding/Spelling:
Variant Vowels
Lesson 3

Getting Ready for a Road Trip

"Wake up, Wendy!" my mom whispered. "We don't want to have a late start."

I jumped right out of bed. I couldn't wait for the day to begin. I grabbed my toothbrush, clean laundry, and my lucky turquoise belt, and shoved them into a bag. I went outside to put my stuff in the car.

My dad seemed annoyed. I asked him what was wrong. He said, "We have enough stuff in this car to stay a week, and we are only staying the weekend!"

Mom and I decided there would be no point in letting anything bother us. We would have to rescue Dad from his bad mood. We didn't want to take away from the excitement of our trip.

Circle and write the word that best completes each sentence.

1. Wendy grabbed some clothes and her _____.

   bamboo   toothbrush   shawl

2. Her lucky belt is decorated with _____.

   turquoise   powder   jewel

3. Wendy also needed clean _____ for the trip.

   oysters   laundry   roosters

4. Her dad seemed _____.

   drawn   appointed   annoyed

5. Dad would need to be _____ from his bad mood.

   rescued   countered   scooped

6. Wendy and her mom made it a _____ to not let anything ruin their trip.

   choose   point   scoop

"Walt Helps Out" • Practice Book
© Harcourt • Grade 5

Name _____

eccentric	be	talked
infuriated	for	dropped
disheartened	some	worried
impassable	to	changing
relented	the	picnicking
faze	her	obeyed
crusaded	of	

1. Many people thought / Susan was eccentric / when she talked / about the right to vote.

2. The women were looking forward / to the meeting, / but it didn't faze them / when the time kept changing.

3. The volunteers / crusaded for the rights of others.

4. The crowd was impassable, / so they came up / with a different plan.

5. Some people would be worried / about the angry crowd.

6. Usually, Susan obeyed / what others told her to do, / but this time / she was infuriated.

7. At last, / the crowd relented / and let her through.

8. Susan dropped her ballot / into the box / without protest.

9. Later that day, / Susan joined several people / picnicking in the park.

10. She was not disheartened / by the day's events.

"When Susan B. Anthony Voted"
• Practice Book
© Harcourt • Grade 5

Read the sentences below. Circle the complete subject and underline the complete predicate.

1. The tired hikers sat down to rest.

2. A large crowd watched the movie.

3. The powerful storm blew through town.

4. The old salesclerk had a hard time hearing.

5. The construction workers built the house.

6. The eager students listened to the teacher.

Read the sentences below. Circle the simple subject and underline the simple predicate.

7. The boy ate all the ice cream.

8. Police officers guarded the museum.

9. The beautiful flowers grew very tall.

10. The entire school sang the song.

11. The tree's leaves fell on the ground.

12. The excited children ran quickly through the leaves.

Word choice can make your writing more effective. Good writers choose their words carefully in order to convey ideas precisely and create a clear picture in the reader's mind. Good writers use vivid words when describing people, places, things, or events to make their ideas come to life.

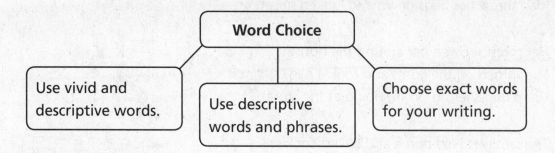

A. Read the sentences below. Underline vivid and descriptive words.

Example   Susan exclaimed, "I am desperate for something to eat!"

1. The ancient stone was put in a special case for viewing.

2. The booming drums could be heard from the street.

3. I walked to the enormous garden to look at the gorgeous plants.

4. The petite child had a high-pitched voice.

5. The lightning flashed and the thunder roared.

B. Read the paragraph below. Underline vivid verbs, circle precise nouns.

Example   The roses fit flawlessly in the canister.

On Friday, I attended the opening of the new library wing. I never envisioned the assortment that would be available there. I saw stories that were mysteries, books about animals, and novels about sports. My imagination began to run wild. I wanted to choose something fascinating to read, but everything caught my eye! I was already anticipating the next time I could come back!

C. On a separate sheet of paper, write a short paragraph about an event you recently attended. Use the previous passage as an example.

"When Susan B. Anthony Voted"
• Practice Book
© Harcourt • Grade 5

Name _____

Circle the letter in front of the sentence that best describes the picture.

1. A   Joan unpacked her bags and began to feel settled.
   B   Joan sat on the couch and began watching TV.
   C   Joan threw her bags down and looked upset.

2. A   Her mom showed her around the house.
   B   She turned off the lights and took a nap.
   C   Her parents left to go shopping at the store.

3. A   The family stayed home and baked cookies.
   B   They were tired, so they all lay down and watched a movie.
   C   Joan's family drove into town and explored their new city.

4. A   They turned around and went straight home.
   B   They stopped and got an ice cream cone.
   C   The family's car broke down.

5. A   Joan's parents showed her the school she would be attending.
   B   They got lost in the town.
   C   Joan shopped for new school clothes.

6. A   Joan was nervous, so she decided not to go to her new school.
   B   Joan began meeting friends right away.
   C   The teacher assigned Joan homework right away.

7. A   Joan baked cookies to bring to her classmates the next day.
   B   Joan played video games after school.
   C   Joan went home and began working on her homework right away.

"When Susan B. Anthony Voted"
• Practice Book
© Harcourt • Grade 5

genial	a	reason
prognostication	are	coach
stricken	he	hurried
dramatically	the	scared
restrain	she	changing
protest		
feverishly		
overcome		
flop		
spectacular		

1. The genial teacher / made a spectacular / prognostication.

2. She acted / dramatically / in the play.

3. The coach restrained her anger / during the student's protest.

4. He practiced / his lines / feverishly.

5. The twins are stricken / with stage fright.

6. They had to / overcome / their fear.

7. Addison was scared / of being a flop.

8. There was a reason / why Ashton / couldn't speak.

9. The actors were busy / changing / into their costumes.

10. The twins hurried / off the stage / at the end.

"Twin Talent" • Practice Book
© Harcourt • Grade 5

Name _____

Write each sentence correctly on the line.

1. Please arrive on time for the party?

   _____

2. Ouch I just got a paper cut.

   _____

3. which book are you going to read first.

   _____

4. throw the ball to first base

   _____

5. My friend moved far away?

   _____

6. Hurray our team just won the game

   _____

7. my brother had the leading role in the play.

   _____

8. Noah helped his sister with her homework!

   _____

"Twin Talent" • Practice Book
© Harcourt • Grade 5

Name _____

**Add the missing subject or predicate to each sentence
fragment to complete the sentence. Then write the complete
sentence correctly.**

1. my dog Daisy

   _____

2. scored the winning point

   _____

3. climbed up the tree

   _____

4. the teacher

   _____

5. wrote a report about the Grand Canyon.

   _____

6. is going to watch the soccer game.

   _____

7. the concert

   _____

8. my sister

   _____

"Twin Talent" • **Practice Book**

Circle the letter in front of the sentence that best describes the picture.

1. A   He is buying a new table.
   B   The table is made of rayon.
   C   He is trying to measure the table.

2. A   The coach is speaking to the actors on the stage.
   B   The actors had not obeyed the coach.
   C   The actor is a fraud.

3. A   The crew is moving the couch off the stage.
   B   The people are buying the couch.
   C   The couch clashed with the curtains.

4. A   The man is standing in front of royalty.
   B   The man is kneeling before royalty.
   C   The man appoints royalty.

5. A   There is a scoop in the crown.
   B   The crown is made of rayon.
   C   There are many jewels in the crown.

6. A   The actor is kneeling on the stage.
   B   The actor hurried off the stage.
   C   The actor is a fraud.

7. A   He is scared.
   B   He is a coach.
   C   He is awfully happy.

8. A   They are acting scared.
   B   They are talking about food.
   C   They are buying tickets.

"Twin Talent" • **Practice Book**
© Harcourt • Grade 5

Name _____

wistful	saw	drizzle
grateful	the	pickle
grim	down	wiggle
raspy	to	gobble
swarmed	over	vehicle
revelers	now	bundle
irresistible	he	

1. With a wistful look, / Ray watched the rain / drizzle down / on the beach.

2. Ray was grateful / to be in a warm boat, / eating a sandwich / and a pickle.

3. He looked / in the ocean / and saw a fish wiggle / through the water.

4. He also saw a large fish / about to gobble up / a smaller one.

5. Ray had gotten over / his raspy throat yesterday, / and now he wanted / to go out.

6. When the rain stopped, / some birds swarmed / around a man.

7. Ray saw some revelers / on the beach, / flying kites.

8. One had a grim look / on his face / as he entered his vehicle / and left the beach.

9. Now / the sun was shining, / and the weather was irresistible.

10. So, / Ray picked up a bundle / of beach toys / and headed down / to the sand.

"Ray and Joan" • Practice Book
© Harcourt • Grade 5

Name _____

Combine each set of sentences, using a compound subject or a compound predicate.

1. Ray likes model boats. Joan likes model boats. Joan's dad likes model boats.

_____

2. Ray lives on a boat in the summer. Ray's parents live on a boat in the summer.

_____

3. Ray swims in the bay. Ray walks along the beach.

_____

4. Ray ate lunch. Ray built a model boat. Ray took a nap.

_____

5. Ray poached a few eggs. Ray ate the eggs.

_____

6. A man was jogging along the coast. His dog was jogging along the coast.

_____

7. Necklaces were displayed at one stall. Pins were displayed there. Rings were displayed there.

_____

8. A woman bought a necklace. She put it on.

_____

9. People listened to music. People flew kites. People waded in the water.

_____

10. Birds were in the air. Kites were in the air. Balloons were in the air.

_____

Name _____

Writers share ideas in their writing. It is important that the ideas have a focus. Then all the details in the writing should focus on the main idea.

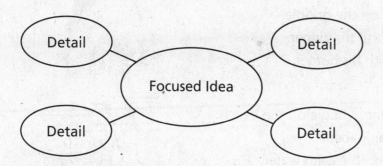

A. Read each broad topic. Then circle the words that best narrow that focus.

Example   **Topic:** Sailboats
Possible Focus: Boats   (Making a Model Sailboat)

1. **Topic:** Seagulls
   Possible Focus: A Seagull's Diet   Water Birds

2. **Topic:** Golden Retrievers
   Possible Focus: Dogs   Training Your Golden Retriever

3. **Topic:** Jogging
   Possible Focus: Exercise   Choosing a Good Running Shoe

B. Read the sentences from *Ray and Joan* and think about the main idea.

Ray watched a sailboat float along. Kids with kites ran on the sand. A man and his dog were jogging along the coast.

Circle the example below that provides another detail to the main idea above.

- Ray wished he had a kite. He had always enjoyed watching other people fly them, but he had never tried it himself.

- Joan gazed out at the beach from her stall at the festival. People were enjoying the day in many different ways.

- Mr. Schultz and his little dog ran along the beach, enjoying the sand and the surf. The little dog had never been happier.

C. On a separate sheet of paper, write a focused idea for the following topic: Summer Vacations. List some details you would like to include for your topic.

"Ray and Joan" • Practice Book

Name _____

Circle the letter in front of the sentence that best describes the picture.

1. **A** Ray's mom cooks dinner on the griddle.
   B Ray has to struggle to finish his dinner.
   C Ray's dad has a pickle with his burger.

2. **A** Ray hears someone playing a bugle on the beach.
   B Ray reads an article in the paper.
   C Ray sees hardly a ripple on the calm water.

3. **A** Ray carries a heavy bundle along the beach.
   B It starts to drizzle as Ray walks on the beach.
   C Ray's vehicle has a flat tire.

4. **A** The man will soon hobble away.
   B Ray thinks the rocks will soon topple over.
   C The man puts a speckle of paint on the top rock.

5. **A** The bells jingle in the wind.
   B The bells hurtle to the ground.
   C The bells are displayed on a spindle.

6. **A** Ray gobbles his burger quickly.
   B Ray's mom does not let him meddle in the kitchen.
   C Ray likes a triple order of cheese on his burger.

7. **A** Ray shuffles his feet when he walks.
   B Ray learns a dance that includes a wiggle.
   C Ray reads an article about dancing.

Name _____

fret	look	excellent
assured	so	terrific
nudged	you	suppose
outlandish	could	common
ruckus	her	message
proclaimed	said	arrange
	your	success

1. Owen's big problem, / he proclaimed to Sara, / was a bump on his nose.

2. "Now don't fret about it, / Owen," / said Sara.

3. "But, Sara," / moaned Owen, / "I will look so outlandish / at the talent show!"

4. Sara assured Owen / that he would not.

5. "You are an excellent juggler, / Owen, / and your show is terrific!"

6. "But don't you suppose / it will cause a ruckus / when everyone sees my nose?" / he asked.

7. "Don't babble about nonsense, / Owen," / said Sara.

8. Sara tried to appeal / to Owen's common sense.

9. At last, / her message nudged him / in the right direction.

10. If he could just arrange / a good costume, / his show would be a success.

"Owen's Big Show" • **Practice Book**
© Harcourt • Grade 5

Identify the underlined parts. Use the words in the box.

> simple sentence   compound subject   run-on sentence
> compound sentence   compound predicate   comma splice

1. <u>Owen liked to juggle he was good at it.</u> _____

2. <u>Owen, Jack, and Sara</u> met in the park to practice their act. _____

3. <u>Jack's dog, Bud, always tagged along with him.</u> _____

4. <u>Owen had an old costume, he thought he'd use it for the show.</u>

   _____

5. <u>Sara played the harmonica, and Jack blew bubbles.</u> _____

6. Bud followed Jack to the park, and he <u>ran and played</u> with some other dogs there.

   _____

7. <u>Sara and Owen</u> performed well. _____

8. <u>Jack joined the two and assisted them.</u> _____

9. <u>Owen called Sara she had a plan.</u> _____

10. <u>The show was saved, for Owen had a plan.</u> _____

Name _____

Good writers focus their ideas. They make sure every detail contributes to the main idea they are focusing on.

Broad Topic
Narrower Topic
More Narrow Topic
Focus

A. Read each broad topic. Then circle the words that provide a more detailed focus.

Example **Topic:** Entertainment

Possible Focus: A History of Music   (Taking Care of Your Clarinet)

1. **Topic:** Talent Show Routines

   Possible Focus: How to Tell a Good Joke   Putting on a Talent Show

2. **Topic:** Trees

   Possible Focus: The Life Cycle of a Willow Tree   Plants of North America

3. **Topic:** Telephones

   Possible Focus: Communication   Taking Photos with Your Cell Phone

4. **Topic:** Bees

   Possible Focus: Treating a Bee Sting   Insects

B. Read the sentences from *Owen's Big Show* and think about the main idea.

Owen had a problem—a big problem. It was there in the middle of his nose! Some insect had bitten him, and the bite had grown into a big, red bump.

Circle the detail below that would contribute to the main idea.

• Owen was planning to do a juggling act for the talent show.

• Sara was a good friend to Owen, and she always knew what to say.

• How could he ever go on stage with this big bump on his nose?

C. On a separate sheet of paper, write three details that would focus on the following topic: Scarecrows.

"Owen's Big Show" • Practice Book
© Harcourt • Grade 5

Read the story. Circle all words with the VCCV pattern.

The radio announcer had an important message. He made an appeal to all the listeners to adopt a pet. Many dogs, he said, were at the kennel owned by the city. Ann asked her dad if they could go, for she wanted to adopt a dog.

"Do you suppose they'll have one you'll like?" he asked.

"Yes, I do!" exclaimed Ann. "A common dog is all I want—nothing fancy."

Soon, Ann and her dad were at the kennel. One little dog—a mutt—looked out at Ann. "What a sweet dog!" said Ann. "It would be terrific if we could get her!"

"Let's see what we can arrange," said her dad.

They talked to the person in charge. She needed to collect a small fee to cover the dog's medical costs so far. Ann's dad paid it, and soon Ann had the dog in her arms.

"Hello, little dog," she cooed. "What an excellent pet you are!" The dog just licked Ann's face.

Circle and write the word that best completes each sentence.

1. The announcer's important _____ is about dogs who need homes.

   letter   message   summary

2. The dogs are kept at a city-owned _____.

   kennel   office   station

3. Ann wants just a _____ dog—nothing fancy.

   puppy   spotted   common

4. Ann thinks it would be _____ if they could get that dog.

   success   slippery   terrific

5. The person in charge has to _____ a small fee.

   arrange   collect   announce

6. Ann is very happy with her _____ little pet.

   excellent   slippery   noisy

crucial	he	furnace
encountered	into	survive
crisis	over	turmoil
persuading	some	identify
maneuvered	they	establish
appealed	the	public
perseverance		
destiny		

1. The men / encountered a crisis / in the Boston port.

2. They used perseverance / to establish / their independence.

3. It was the destiny / of some / to survive the turmoil.

4. They needed to / identify the tea / on the boat.

5. They maneuvered the tea chests / over the side / and into the sea.

6. Sam Adams / was persuading others / to stop paying taxes.

7. He appealed / to the public / to stop drinking tea.

8. It was crucial / that the tea / not be taxed.

9. The colonists / had only a fireplace, / not a furnace.

10. The entire shipment / of tea / went into the water.

Name _____

Underline the prepositional phrase in each sentence. Circle the
preposition. Insert a comma after a prepositional phrase if it is
needed. Write the object of the preposition on the line.

1. The troops moved forward at midnight. _____

2. During the field trip we stopped and ate lunch. _____

3. Across the lake, we could see the campsite. _____

4. They drove slowly through the woods because it was dark. _____

5. Around the corner there is a grocery store. _____

6. Jeff went swimming in the lake. _____

7. Ms. Jenson was the principal of the school. _____

8. Craig played catch with some friends. _____

9. Joan looked over her shoulder to see if anyone was following her. _____

10. The officer served in 2002. _____

11. Many changes were made during that time. _____

12. After the last bell the crowds went home. _____

"Tea Time in Boston" • Practice Book
© Harcourt • Grade 5

When writing a biography, the author states important facts or details about the person's life in the order in which they happened. Look at the diagram below to see how a biography is organized.

A topic sentence introduces the person.	→	Details, facts, and dates tell about the person.	→	Time words show sequence of events.	→	A conclusion sums up the person's life.

A. Read the topic sentence. Then put an X by the sentences that support it.

Topic sentence: Lord North was the Prime Minister of England.

_____ In 1773, he worked to pass the Tea Act.

_____ He repealed four of the five taxes on the American Colonies in 1770.

_____ The British taxed things such as sugar, paper, and tea.

_____ After the Boston Tea Party, North ordered the harbor closed.

B. Read this paragraph. Underline the topic sentence. Circle the words that show the order of events.

Sam Adams was a busy man. When he was young, he studied law, tried to start a business, and worked as a tax collector. Later, he seems to have worked full time to persuade the colonists to break their ties with England. Adams used his talents to write letters in newspapers. The letters told about how badly the British were treating the colonists. In 1773, Adams was one of the men who planned the Boston Tea Party. Three years later, he eagerly signed the Declaration of Independence. Adams devoted nearly his whole life to this new country called the United States.

C. On a separate sheet of paper, write a one-paragraph biography about a family member. Use the same structure as the paragraph about Sam Adams.

Do what the sentences tell you to do.

1. Write on the sign on the tree: Rob's Picnic.

2. Draw a napkin at each of the four places at the table.

3. Draw a plastic spoon on each napkin.

4. Draw a festive decoration on the table.

5. Draw a bowl of pretzels on the table.

6. Color the blanket red.

7. Draw a chipmunk on a tree branch.

8. Identify the falcon and place a circle around it.

9. Color the bike helmet on the blanket blue.

10. Circle the racket on the blanket.

Now circle all the words that have the VCCV pattern.

Name _____

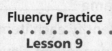

scholars	a	congress
specialized	could	complex
gesture	do	contribute
envisioned	to	conclude
proportion	how	concrete
resisted	the	technique
	they	accomplish

1. The scholars resisted / a plan / to remove the tiles.

2. They specialized / in art / of the early 1900s.

3. The members / of the congress / envisioned / a restored / state capitol.

4. The artist knew how / to do / the technique.

5. It was a gesture / of good will / to contribute / the painting.

6. The marble tiles were / in perfect proportion.

7. They could not / accomplish the work / in one week.

8. It took / many weeks / to conclude / the complex project.

9. Hans Scharff / did not complain / about his job.

10. The tiles were set / in concrete / when he / was finished.

"The Tile Floor" • **Practice Book**
© Harcourt • Grade 5

Identify each item as a phrase, dependent clause, or
independent clause.

1. The students took a tour of Williamsburg, Virginia.

_____

2. a group of friends

_____

3. although they were sisters

_____

4. the winning point at the soccer game

_____

5. The tournament was very exciting.

_____

6. when Ann scored the goal

_____

**Underline the independent clause and circle the dependent clause in each complex
sentence below.**

7. When the movie was over, we went out for dinner.

8. We got in line for the tickets although it was long.

9. Because her favorite color is purple, she wore a lavender dress.

10. We missed the best part since we were late.

"The Tile Floor" • Practice Book
© Harcourt • Grade 5

Name _____

In **organizing a summary**, the important ideas or events that support the main idea should be restated in chronological order. Look at the graphic organizer below to see how a summary is developed.

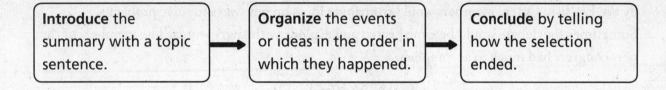

| **Introduce** the summary with a topic sentence. | → | **Organize** the events or ideas in the order in which they happened. | → | **Conclude** by telling how the selection ended. |

A. Read the paragraph.

In 1975, the tile floor in the California State Capitol needed to be restored. The tile floor was located on the upper hall floor. It included more than 600,000 tiles. First, the floor was scored and then cut into parts, like a puzzle. After this was completed, the parts were pasted onto big boards. Next, an artist took the tiles off the boards and cleaned them, one by one. The cleaning took a long time. Then, the tiles were set back onto the floor, in the same order as before.

B. Follow the directions below.

1. Underline the sentence in the paragraph that would be used to write the topic sentence of a summary.

2. Circle the words that show chronological order.

3. Write a detail that you could leave out of a summary.

_____

C. On a separate sheet of paper, use the details you noted in Part B to write a summary of the paragraph above. Be sure to include a concluding statement that tells how the restoration turned out.

"The Tile Floor" • **Practice Book**
© Harcourt • Grade 5

Read the story. Circle all words with the VCCCV pattern.

Even before the colonists won their freedom from the English,
they set up a congress to protect their rights and interests. During the meetings in congress, there
was an expression of opinions on complex issues. People would complain about unfair treatment
by the English. Often, members would contribute ideas on new ways to solve problems.
Sometimes the debate would become heated and explode with angry words. The members of the
new congress had much to accomplish.

Circle and write the word that best completes each sentence.

1. To protect their rights and interests, the colonists created a _____.

   technique   congress   fortress

2. The congress was a place for the _____ of different opinions.

   expression   impression   explosion

3. Sometimes, the issues raised were _____.

   concrete   complex   congress

4. Members of the congress would _____ about unfair treatment.

   conclude   contribute   complain

5. Sometimes, members would _____ ideas on how to solve problems.

   contribute   concrete   conclude

6. During the meetings, there was much to _____.

   publish   complain   accomplish

eminent	my	struggle
charity	could	hurricane
modest	have	terrific
disgruntled	some	message
inadequate	down	excellent
aghast		
dismayed		
amends		
absentminded		
concoction		

1. The disgruntled victims / of the latest hurricane / struggle with inadequate supplies.

2. The telethon organizers / hope to help them / in more than / just modest ways.

3. They have asked / an eminent chef / to contribute his talents / to their fund-raising show.

4. The charity event will begin / in a few minutes.

5. The absentminded chef / has not shown up yet, / and the organizers are aghast / at this development.

6. Dawn tells them / not to be dismayed.

7. She says she can cook up / some interesting concoction / just as easily / as Chef Mark.

8. "My grandma was a terrific cook, / and she passed down her wisdom / to me."

9. The announcer amends her message / to the audience.

10. She says that Chef Mark / will be replaced / by another excellent cook.

Grammar:
Compound
Subjects and
Predicates, Simple
and Compound
Sentences

Lesson 10

Name _____

Circle the subjects. Underline the predicates. Identify each as a *compound subject, compound predicate, simple sentence* or *compound sentence*.

1. Claire frosted a cake, and Jerry made some cookies.

   _____

2. Claire's creation was an apple and nutmeg cake.

   _____

3. Claire and Jerry enjoyed preparing the desserts.

   _____

4. Jerry washed and dried the bowls and spoons.

   _____

Rewrite these sentences. Use compound subjects, compound predicates, or compound sentences.

5. Claire likes to bake. Jerry likes to bake.

   _____

6. Claire cut the cake. Claire served the cake.

   _____

7. They entered their creations in the baking contest. Neither of them won a prize.

   _____

8. They like to make desserts. I volunteer to taste them.

   _____

"Hurricane Turkey" • Practice Book
© Harcourt • Grade 5

Name _____

Identify each item as a *phrase*, an *independent clause*, a *dependent clause*, or a *complex sentence*. Add a comma, if needed.

1. After baseball practice was over. _____

2. Everyone walked to the restaurant. _____

3. About the same time we arrived it started to rain.

    _____

4. For a long time. _____

5. Whenever Patsy eats pepperoni pizza. _____

6. Because Patsy was very hungry she ordered two slices.

    _____

7. Christopher's favorite pizza is black olive and mushroom.

    _____

8. With extra pineapple and ham. _____

9. Under the seat of his chair. _____

10. Although we ordered several pizzas. _____

"Hurricane Turkey" • **Practice Book**
© Harcourt • Grade 5

Circle the letter in front of the sentence that best describes the picture.

1. A   Brian looks over the merchandise.
    B   Brian belongs to an orchestra.
    C   Brian will arrange to make all the shirts.

2. A   Tessa carries a bundle on her back.
    B   Tessa will conclude her tennis practice soon.
    C   The instructor observes Tessa's swimming technique.

3. A   The man's journey is just starting.
    B   The vehicle has a flat tire.
    C   The man's problems will triple.

4. A   The people struggle to repair the town.
    B   The hurricane pounds the town.
    C   The town is in excellent condition.

5. A   They whisper secrets.
    B   They will accomplish great things.
    C   They have a terrific time.

6. A   She will hurtle the pancakes into the trashcan.
    B   She sees a hurricane coming.
    C   When the pancakes are golden, they'll be ready.

7. A   Cindy takes a message.
    B   Cindy will rush to the hospital.
    C   Cindy's expression is sad.

Strategic Intervention · Practice Book
© Harcourt · Grade 5

inflammable	a	balance
dignified	because	closet
rowdy	of	decent
seldom	out	eleven
conducted	the	minute
shatter	into	novel
broached		ocean

1. Because of the storm, / the ship / was off balance.

2. We were afraid / that things would shatter / if the ship broached.

3. The ship / came out of the storm / and into calm waters.

4. We had a decent cabin / with a big closet.

5. The dignified staff / conducted many activities / on the ship.

6. Eleven students / read the novel / for class.

7. The inflammable items / were removed / from the ship.

8. The weather could change / in a minute.

9. People seldom seemed / to get rowdy / on the ship.

10. The ship / crossed the ocean / in eleven days.

Name _____

Circle the common nouns and underline the proper nouns in the sentences.

1. Sam lives near the school.

2. Karen ate a salad for lunch.

3. The Grand Canyon is in the state of Arizona.

4. The girls played tennis in Jackson Park.

5. The concert was on Saturday.

Use abbreviations as you rewrite each item.

6. Doctor Lois Whelan _____

7. 205 Cherry Street _____

8. Mister Frank Liston _____

9. William Craswell, Junior _____

10. Sunrise Highway _____

"My Home Is Shipshape" • **Practice Book**
© Harcourt • Grade 5

Name _____

Good writers use a variety of sentence types and lengths to make their writing interesting. Use a variety of simple, compound, and complex sentences for effective writing.

Read what you have written.	→	Look for short, choppy sentences.	→	Combine two sentences into a longer sentence.

A. Write a new sentence that combines each pair of sentences.

1. I couldn't find my shoes. I looked for them under the bed.

_____

2. I had one pair of clean socks. I realized that I would have do laundry.

_____

3. I got dressed for school. I ate my breakfast.

_____

B. Read the passage.

(1) We visited the place where William Shakespeare was born. (2) He lived in a town called Stratford-Upon-Avon. (3) The town is filled with stone cottages and thatched-roof houses, but there are modern buildings, too. (4) Because Shakespeare was such an important playwright, there is a large theater dedicated to his work. (5) I saw a play there.

Identify each kind of sentence in the passage.

4. Underline the compound sentence.

5. Circle a sentence that contains a dependent clause.

6. Rewrite Sentence 5 so it includes more descriptive details.

_____

C. On another sheet of paper, write three or four sentences to describe a place where you learn. Use a variety of sentence types.

Name _____

Circle the letter in front of the sentence that best describes the picture.

1. **A** Our ship set sail on the ocean.
   B Eleven passengers bought a ticket.
   C The ship has no radar.

2. **A** Sandy was enjoying her novel.
   B Eleven books were stacked on the table.
   C The editor found many errors in the text.

3. **A** The meeting would only take a minute.
   B They met to define the rules.
   C The meeting was private.

4. **A** Jake is a fanatic about race cars.
   B Jake has a great sense of humor.
   C Jake pretends he is not bored.

5. **A** Someone gave Maria a present.
   B Maria lost her balance and fell.
   C Maria put her clothes away in the closet.

6. **A** The captain uses radar to plot the ship's course.
   B The crew brought a report to the captain.
   C The captain was afraid a second storm would hit.

7. **A** Their trip was the basis of a new movie.
   B His model of a sailing ship is complete.
   C They realized that finally they had decent weather.

"My Home Is Shipshape" • Practice Book
© Harcourt • Grade 5

Name _____

adjust	some	reconsider
residents	the	retake
specimens	they	nonproductive
recoil	to	unable
pesky	was	nonexistent
debris	were	undesirable
internal		unwise

1. Some specimens / recoil / when you / examine them.

2. The shell / of the crab / protects its internal organs.

3. The pollution / in the water / creates an undesirable habitat.

4. Some people felt / the water problems / were nonexistent.

5. The residents were unable / to convince them.

6. It was unwise / to hold such / a nonproductive meeting.

7. They chose to / retake the photographs / of the debris.

8. Such a pesky problem / needed to be solved.

9. They all decided / to reconsider the project.

10. In time, / the wildlife would adjust / to its new habitat.

"Rock Hounds on the Sound"
• **Practice Book**
© Harcourt • Grade 5

Name _____

**Identify the underlined noun in each sentence as singular or
plural. If the underlined noun is singular, write its plural form
on the line.**

1. We looked for the unpacked box. _____

2. The class exchanged letters. _____

3. Steven and Jay are brothers. _____

4. Joan found the blueberries. _____

5. I know the person who designed the new school library. _____

Write the irregular plural form of the underlined noun in each sentence.

6. The man worked in Seattle. _____

7. The ingredients include tomato. _____

8. They are going to attach the shelf to the wall. _____

9. Gabe lost his front tooth. _____

10. The deer stood still. _____

11. The woman went to the event. _____

12. This event honored the hero for bravery. _____

"Rock Hounds on the Sound"
• **Practice Book**
© Harcourt • Grade 5

Name _____

Writers use many different types of **sentences** to keep the reader interested. The graphic organizer below shows many ways to write effective sentences.

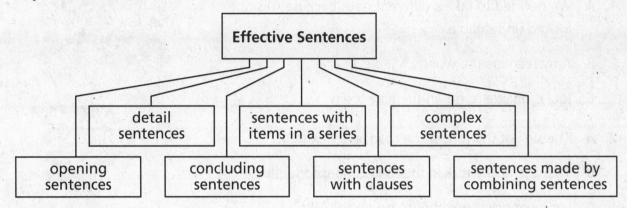

A. Read this passage.

  Hermit crabs are fascinating creatures to study. They can live outside at the shoreline. Some live indoors as pets. Unlike other crabs, hermit crabs do not have their own shells. Instead, they hide for protection in shells that other animals once used. Hermit crabs have only two claws. They use their huge claw to block an attack by a predator. They use their other claw, which is smaller, for gathering food and eating it. As hermit crabs grow, they shed their outer skeleton and grow a new one! Hermit crabs have many unusual features that help them survive.

B. Follow the directions, using the paragraph above.

1. Put a box around the opening sentence.

2. Underline the sentence that contrasts or tells how things are different.

3. Rewrite the following sentences as one sentence:

   They can live outside at the shoreline. Some live indoors as pets.

   _____

   _____

C. On a separate sheet of paper, write four sentences about another animal that lives in the water. Use at least one simple, one complex, and one compound sentence.

Name _____

Decoding/Spelling:
**Words with
Prefixes**
re-, un-, non-
• • • • • • • • •
Lesson 12

Circle the letter in front of the sentence that best describes the picture.

1. A   We decided to take a different path because this one looked undesirable.

    B   Amy reenters the woods.

    C   Joel is unable to go on the hike today.

2. A   The sign at the fork in the road is nonexistent.

    B   The sign at the fork in the road is nonproductive.

    C   Jan reconsiders whether to go on the hike.

3. A   Their secret is nonexistent.

    B   Their secret is untold.

    C   It is unwise to tell a secret.

4. A   For lunch, Amy ate a taco filled with refried beans.

    B   Amy wants to remake lunch.

    C   Amy ate a nondairy meal for lunch.

5. A   Juan and Debbie were uninformed about rowboats.

    B   Juan and Debbie repaint the rowboat a different color.

    C   The rowboat is nonflammable.

6. A   Many campers replant the flowers outdoors.

    B   Larry will retake the photograph of his flowers.

    C   It is unwise for the campers to move the plants.

7. A   During the hike, my friend Jeff spotted a kinglet.

    B   Larry retakes photographs from different angles.

    C   The nest is nonflammable.

"Rock Hounds on the Sound"
• Practice Book
© Harcourt • Grade 5

bellowing	a	divisible
outcast	their	irresistible
reputation	new	appointment
betrayed	to	argument
yearning	said	apartment
withered	was	judgment
unfathomable		ageless

1. The captains / had an argument, / and both / felt betrayed.

2. Their new apartment / could be seen / from the harbor.

3. Luckily for the passengers, / the food was divisible.

4. Everyone found / the new ship / to be irresistible.

5. The wind / was so strong, / and its power was unfathomable.

6. The passengers / made a judgment about the captain / that made him feel / like an outcast.

7. The captain looked ageless, / for he wasn't even slightly withered.

8. The ship needed to be fixed, / so the captain / made an appointment / at the harbor.

9. A passenger said / he had a reputation / for making bellowing sounds.

10. The captain was yearning / for the ocean waves / to calm down.

Name _____

Read the sentences. Circle the singular possessive nouns and underline the plural possessive nouns.

1. Lisa's favorite movie changes every week.

2. The teachers' meeting was cancelled.

3. The birds' nests are falling apart.

4. The men's travel plans were interrupted by rain.

5. Jared's shirt has blue and white stripes.

Read the sentences. Correct the mistakes and rewrite the sentence correctly.

6. Sarahs shoe is untied.

_____

7. The puppies bowl was empty.

_____

8. Sandras dress lost a button.

_____

9. The cars engine rattled in a strange way.

_____

10. Many trees leaves turned bright colors.

_____

"Salty on the High Seas" • Practice Book
© Harcourt • Grade 5

Name _____

Conventions in writing refer to the use of correct grammar and punctuation. It is important for writers to use correct spelling, grammar, punctuation, and capitalization to help readers understand what they are trying to say.

A. Read the sentences. Rewrite the sentence correctly on the line below.

1. do you really like runing on the playground

   _____

2. My parents are both from florida

   _____

3. Monica james and carlos are all in the play.

   _____

B. Read the paragraph. Cross out the mistakes. Then rewrite the paragraph correctly.

My dad is the coolest person i know. Hes really tall and has dark brown hair. My dad is skinny because he allways exercises. My dad wares glasses because he can't see without them. My dad is careing, funny, and loveing. These are all of the reasons he is also my best friend.

_____

_____

_____

_____

C. Think of a character from a book you have read. On a separate sheet of paper, write a description of the character. Make sure to use proper writing conventions.

Name _____

Decoding/Spelling:
Words with
Suffixes -able,
-ible, -less, -ment

Lesson 13

Read the story below. Circle all of the words with the suffixes
-able, -ible, -less, -ment.

It was a rainy weekend and we didn't have much to do. My mom decided to make an appointment to tour our local art museum. I wasn't going to get into an argument about it, since getting out of the house sounded fantastic to me! We left our apartment and headed downtown.

When we arrived, I looked at everything in amazement. I hadn't ever seen anything like it! I saw a priceless masterpiece by a famous artist. I saw gems, statues, and paintings. I thought everything was very interesting.

Before we left, we stopped at the cafeteria. I ate a slice of chocolate cake that was irresistible. I asked my mom if we could go back sometime soon. She said, "To tour the museum or to eat the chocolate cake?"

I said, "Both!" My mom just laughed in amusement.

Circle and write the word that best completes each sentence.

1. We made an _____ to tour the museum.

   arrangement   apartment   appointment

2. There was no _____ from me about this idea!

   arrangement   argument   irresistible

3. I looked at the displays in _____.

   amazement   argument   apartment

4. The masterpiece by the famous artist is _____.

   priceless   dispensible   aimless

5. The chocolate cake was simply _____.

   resentment   responsible   irresistible

6. My mom laughed in _____.

   amazement   embarrassment   amusement

elongates	a	discover
elastic	some	frozen
rigid	the	general
accumulate	they	hidden
underlying	to	proper
intricate	when	inventor
vanish		
replenishing		

1. A water droplet / elongates / as it slides / down a glass.

2. Water / can accumulate / to form a puddle.

3. Water / appears to vanish / when it evaporates.

4. An underlying layer / of frozen water / is stored / beneath the peaks.

5. Some snowflakes / have intricate shapes.

6. The opposite / of elastic / is rigid.

7. Water is always / replenishing itself.

8. They may discover / water hidden / in unexpected places.

9. In general, / life on our planet / needs water to survive.

10. The inventor / developed the proper procedure / for purifying water.

Name _____

**Circle the pronoun and underline its antecedent in each pair
of sentences.**

1. The raindrops accumulated on the steps of the front porch.
   They formed a puddle.

2. Jordan left the backpack at home.
   Jordan went back home to get it.

3. Nancy wrote a letter to the mayor.
   She mailed it the next day.

4. Joshua called some friends to go skating.
   He met them at the rink.

5. The doctor examined the patient.
   She said that the patient was healthy.

**Circle the pronoun. Draw an arrow to the antecedent. Write the sentence correctly so
the pronoun and antecedent agree.**

6. Pablo and Mary missed the bus, so both of us had to walk.

   _____

7. Caroline asked if they could be next to give her report to the class.

   _____

8. The teacher asked the students if I had any questions.

   _____

9. My aunt bought earrings and lost it.

   _____

10. My brother and I couldn't go to the movie because they worked on Saturday.

   _____

"Water on Our Planet" • Practice Book

It is important for writers to use correct conventions when writing.
Correct conventions make writing easier for readers to understand.

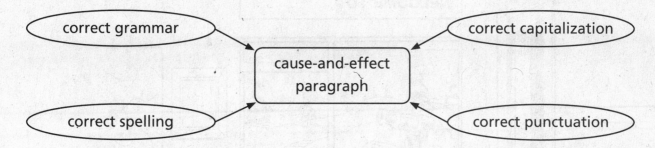

A. Read each sentence. Circle the capitalization errors. Underline the punctuation errors. Draw a line through any misspelled words. Then write each sentence correctly on the line.

1. when energy heats up frozen water: it terns into a liquid.

_____

2. as a drop of Water drips down a window, it elongats,

_____

3. if it is cold outside than water will turn to frost.

_____

B. Read the paragraph.

   Have you ever thought about why clouds appear a certain way? Water droplets that forms them are different sizes. When the water droplets are small, then a cloud looks brighter at the top and darker at the bottom. Larger droplets allow more sunlight to pass through, smaller droplets scatter the way the sun passes through the cloud.

1. Underline the comma splice. Write it correctly.

_____

2. Put a box around the error in subject-verb agreement.

3. Put a star next to the signal words that show cause and effect.

C. On your own paper, write a sentence that shows cause and effect. Proofread for correct grammar, spelling, capitalization, and punctuation.

WELCOME TO

Letter from the Mayor

Theater Listings

Brochures

Do what the sentences tell you to do.

1. Complete the welcome sign by filling in the name of your state capitol.

2. Put a box around the letter from the mayor.

3. Draw a cup and saucer on the table. Color them blue.

4. Draw a barrel next to the table. Color it brown.

5. Circle the newsletter that has the headline "Theater Listings."

6. A frozen icicle hangs outside. Draw it hanging from the roof.

7. Color the cannon gray.

8. Draw a sign that says "Line for musical tickets starts here.

9. A picture of a general hangs on the wall. Draw his picture in the frame.

10. Draw an arrow pointing to something that seems hidden in the closet.

Now, circle the Spelling Words.

Name _____

recount	there	ocean
uninhabitable	because	unwise
sustain	to	argument
monotonous	you	reclaim
endeavor	the	enemy
dwell		
brimming		
teeming		
parched		
sorrowful		

1. This story will recount / our endeavor / to reclaim the beach.

2. Our trip to the ocean / was sorrowful, / because the beach had / so much trash.

3. The tide pools should have been / teeming with life, / but they were filled with trash.

4. Animals should be able / to dwell at the beach, / but it was uninhabitable.

5. There was some argument / about how to start.

6. We decided / it was unwise / to work alone.

7. The trash strewn / over the beach / was our enemy.

8. It was monotonous / to pick up trash / day after day.

9. We were parched, / so we got cups / brimming with water.

10. We were proud to see / that the tide pools / now sustained life.

"Grandma's Tale" • **Practice Book**
© Harcourt • Grade 5

Proofread each sentence, and write it correctly.

1. The Smiths visited paris, france, on Vacation.

   _____

2. The Principal, mrs. Wong, invited the womans.

   _____

3. Dad put the bunnys back in the hutch.

   _____

4. On mondays, the fishes need to be fed.

   _____

5. I have always wanted to meet the astronautes at nasa.

   _____

Now write each noun from the sentences above in the correct column. Each noun will be used twice.

Common	Proper	Singular	Plural

"Grandma's Tale" • **Practice Book**
© Harcourt • Grade 5

Name _____

A. Complete each sentence by adding a possessive noun that means the same as the phrase in parentheses.

1. The teacher asked for _____. (paper of Tawanda)

2. Put some water in the _____. (bowls of the dogs)

3. I saw wildflowers in the _____. (meadow of the deer)

4. Can you find the _____? (shoes of the boys)

5. Did you get the _____? (food of the cat)

B. Underline each pronoun and circle its antecedent or antecedents.

6. Ben was late in turning in his homework.

7. Tabitha and Christina worked on their project.

8. The cats put their muddy paws on the couch.

9. Adammi put on her costume before the play.

10. Tyler and Tanner wished for their flashlights.

"Grandma's Tale" • **Practice Book**
© Harcourt • Grade 5

Read the story. Then circle the letter of the answer that makes each sentence below tell about the story.

The Savoy Theater, next to the capitol, is the oldest theater in town. Unfortunately, it has become very rundown. It was so rickety that some people thought it was unwise to let it stand. The mayor asked the city to reconsider knocking it down. He said that history is priceless, and the theater was an important part of our city's history. There was an argument between both sides. Finally, the demolition company agreed that if we could raise the money to reclaim the site, it would not be knocked down. We started a campaign called "Save the Savoy." We asked for donations. To be honest, I thought we would never meet our goal. Yet, to everyone's amazement, we raised the funds in under a month. When the mayor cut the ribbon, the theater reopened six months later. At the party, everyone enjoyed popcorn, a movie, and a piece of our city's history.

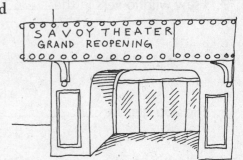

1. Where was the theater located?
   A next to the mayor's office
   B next to the construction company
   C next to the capitol
   D next to the author's house

2. Why did the mayor ask the city to reconsider knocking down the theater?
   A because history is priceless
   B because they need theaters in town
   C because he owned the theater
   D because it was famous

3. What was the slogan for the campaign?
   A "Theaters are priceless"
   B "Save our history!"
   C "The Savoy is Super!"
   D "Save the Savoy!"

4. What was amazing about the campaign?
   A The theater was still standing.
   B They raised the money in a month.
   C The mayor agreed to help.
   D The demolition company stopped working.

5. Who cut the ribbon?
   A the general
   B the mayor
   C the author
   D the owner

6. How were they able to reclaim the site?
   A The mayor proposed a new law to protect it.
   B They had a large protest to stop the demolition.
   C They raised the money to repair the theater.
   D They got volunteers to repair the building.

Name _____

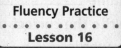
tempted	said	inaccurate
insights	their	impossible
essence	new	illegible
indication	to	injustice
proposed	was	irreplaceable
instinct	what	impolite
baffled	would	

1. It would be inaccurate / to say that Joyce / did not run well.

2. In fact, / she ran so well / that it was almost impossible / to beat her.

3. It was impolite / and an injustice when / Joyce's brother teased her!

4. Joyce was / almost tempted / to complain / to their parents.

5. When Roy read / about a new track star / in the newspaper, / he was quite baffled.

6. The sports writer / shared her insights / about a runner / named SJ.

7. The illegible caption / in the paper / did not give any indication / of who SJ really was.

8. Roy's instinct / told him that / there was more / to this story.

9. The news story said / that SJ was the essence / of a good athlete.

10. The sports writer proposed / that the irreplaceable SJ / would lead the team / to victory.

"Teamwork" • Practice Book
© Harcourt • Grade 5

Name _____

Write the correct pronoun to replace the underlined word or words.

1. Janet has been training for the race. _____

2. Janet and Joey have been training together. _____

3. The coach gives Janet and Joey some good tips. _____

4. Joey bought some running shoes. They were too big for Joey. _____

5. Joey will return the shoes to the store. _____

6. Mr. Martinez ordered a salad for lunch. _____

7. He shared his dessert with Janet and Joey. _____

Write _I_ or _me_ to complete each sentence.

8. Don and _____ attended the race.

9. Carl saved seats for Don and _____.

10. _____ wanted to see if Janet would win.

11. Janet did not disappoint Don and _____.

12. She came in first, and Don and _____ cheered until we were hoarse.

13. _____ decided to celebrate with a pizza.

14. Janet, Don, and _____ had a great time.

Tell students that a writer's **voice** is the way the writer makes the characters and events in a story come to life. Writers often use viewpoint to express how they think and feel about a subject.

| Viewpoint (way of looking at the subject) thoughts, feelings | **Viewpoint** and **Point of View** are parts of a writer's **voice.** | **Point of View** first person, third person |

A. Read the given viewpoint for each sentence. Underline the words or phrases that support the viewpoint.

Example Viewpoint: Amusement

Diane held back a giggle as she watched the monkey's antics.

1. Viewpoint: Favorable

   Brad preferred the soothing coolness of the beach to the heat of the city.

2. Viewpoint: Annoyance

   The ear-splitting screech of the leaf-blower disturbed Henry's nap.

3. Viewpoint: Tempting

   The shiny satins and glittering beads seemed to call out to Marsha, "Buy me!"

B. Read the paragraph. Cross out the sentence that does *not* support the viewpoint.

   Joyce was very angry with her brother. He just didn't seem to respect her the way he should. He never said, "Good job!" when she won a race. He never had a word of encouragement for her. He was very proud of her. All her brother ever did was tease her because he could run faster. He didn't even recognize that it was because he was bigger!

C. Now imagine that Joyce is very pleased with the way her brother treats her. Rewrite the paragraph to show her viewpoint. Use another sheet of paper.

Name _____

Circle the letter in front of the sentence that best describes the picture.

1. A   The black cat is irreplaceable.
    B   Both cats are impolite.
    C   The white cat is inactive.

2. A   The scale shows an imbalance.
    B   The scale is ineffective.
    C   The scale is illegal.

3. A   Ken is illiterate.
    B   Ken's aim is inaccurate.
    C   The dart board is irreplaceable.

4. A   A tadpole is an immature frog.
    B   A tadpole is an irregular frog.
    C   A tadpole is an invalid frog.

5. A   Emily's printing is irrelevant.
    B   Emily's printing is still imperfect.
    C   Emily's printing is impolite.

6. A   It is impossible that it will rain.
    B   The weather forecast is indefinite.
    C   Rain would be irrelevant.

7. A   Tina's mom is independent.
    B   Tina's mom enjoys inaction.
    C   Tina's mom is a bit impatient.

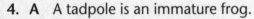
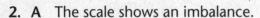

"Teamwork" • Practice Book
© Harcourt • Grade 5

hiatus	from	attendant
embarked	said	hesitant
unimaginable	the	resistant
extravagant	to	insistent
gourmet	was	urgent
throng		pioneer
precarious		artist
		technician

1. Shawna was hesitant / about the trip, / but her mom said / to think of it / as a hiatus from chores.

2. "Don't be so resistant / to change," / said her mom.

3. "Pretend you're a pioneer / exploring a new land," / she went on.

4. "I hate to be insistent, / but I think / you'll enjoy yourself / at Gran's."

5. Shawna embarked on the trip, / even though it was unimaginable / to her / that she'd enjoy it.

6. A throng of people / boarded the plane, / each with an urgent desire / for a window seat.

7. The flight attendant / helped everyone get seated / and calmed them down.

8. Later, / she served gourmet snacks / from a precarious tray / that almost toppled over.

9. At Gran's farm / later that day, / Shawna had an extravagant meal.

10. "You're not a mere food technician, but a food artist!" / Shawna exclaimed.

Circle and write the correct pronoun to complete each sentence.

1. Mrs. Shaw does _____ own gardening.

   her   his   herself

2. Miss Dawson has always wanted a dog, so she finally got one for _____.

   hers   her   herself

3. Jake and Ted forgot _____ jackets today.

   their   theirs   themselves

4. Molly and Michelle fixed _____ a nice picnic.

   herself   hers   themselves

5. The lobster stuck _____ claw behind the rock.

   its   itself   their

6. Roger bought a gift for _____ mother on her birthday.

   himself   his   yours

7. "Paul and Josh, you should give _____ a big pat on the back for what you've done."

   your   yourself   yourselves

8. Carla takes care of her pets _____.

   themselves   herself   hers

9. I can do it _____, thank you!

   myself   mine   ourselves

10. This book isn't mine—it's _____.

    her   herself   hers

"Rained Out at Gran's" • Practice Book
© Harcourt • Grade 5

A writer's **voice** is the unique way in which he or she presents the characters and events in a story. A character's words and actions help reveal his or her personality.

Characters' words reveal what they are like.

Voice

Dialogue between characters seems natural and true-to-life.

A. Read this passage. Look for details that reveal what the characters are like.

Paula: Come on, Shawn! Don't be so slow! We'll be late!

Shawn: Just a minute, Paula. I have to check on the pets.

Paula: I already did that, Shawn. They're fine. Let's go.

Shawn: But I want to be sure. Last time you forgot to fill up their water bowl.

Paula: Oh, they were fine, Shawn. Don't be so fussy!

Shawn: I just want to make sure they'll be all right. It'll just take a minute.

B. Identify details from the passage that reveal the writer's voice.

1. What do you know about Paula's personality? Underline the words in the passage that prove this.

_____

_____

2. What do you know about Shawn's personality? Circle the words in the passage that prove this.

_____

_____

C. On a separate sheet of paper, write four lines of dialogue in your own voice about a job that needs to be done.

"Rained Out at Gran's" • **Practice Book**
© Harcourt • Grade 5

Name _____

Decoding/Spelling:
Suffixes *-ant, -ent,*
-eer, -ist, -ian
· · · · · · · · · ·
Lesson 17

Read the story. Circle all words with the suffixes *-ant, -ent, -eer,*
-ist, **and** *-ian.*

As a volunteer at the animal shelter, Saul watched carefully what each technician did. He observed as they gave the animals the urgent care they needed. One technician was practically an artist at his job. He knew that the animals were dependent on their human caregivers. Saul enjoyed being at the animal shelter. But he was hesitant to apply for a real job there.

"Why not try?" asked his friend Dawn. "The last applicant was not as qualified as you. You might have a better chance than you think."

"OK, Dawn, I'll give it a try. But I'm not too expectant that I'll be hired."

Circle and write the word that best completes each sentence.

1. Saul was working as a _____ at the animal shelter.

    technician   pioneer   volunteer

2. Saul watched as each _____ worked with the animals.

    servant   technician   attendant

3. Some of the animals were in _____ need of care.

    urgent   hesitant   defiant

4. All the animals were _____ on their human caregivers.

    dependent   insistent   indulgent

5. Saul wanted a job, but he was _____ to apply for one.

    resistant   expectant   hesitant

6. Saul was not very _____ that he'd be hired.

    defiant   expectant   insistent

compartments	was	curious
invasion	said	gracious
phobia	you	dangerous
swayed	their	anxious
vetoed	what's	spontaneous
wispy	there	ridiculous
	were	
	do	

1. Dennis had a phobia / about speaking in public, / whether the speech was spontaneous / or planned.

2. When his partners said / he should narrate a slideshow, / he tried to be gracious / as he vetoed the idea.

3. "It's not dangerous," / said Marla, / "and no one will hurt you!"

4. "I know," said Dennis, / "but it just makes me feel / nervous and anxious."

5. Someone, however, / had to tell the class / about the compartments / where the Bantam hens nested.

6. Bantam hens / did not like a sudden invasion / of their space.

7. Someone had to tell the class / about the wispy tails / of the beautiful chickens.

8. Nina was curious because / she didn't understand / what was so scary.

9. Dennis knew / he sounded ridiculous, / but he didn't know / what else to say.

10. The girls thought / that Dennis could not be swayed, / and they were at a loss / about what to do.

"Dennis the Chicken Man"
• Practice Book
© Harcourt • Grade 5

Name _____

Circle and write the word that best completes each sentence.

1. Snow covered _____ ground.

   a   an   the

2. Dan bought _____ new pair of skis.

   worse   an   a

3. Paul had _____ excited feeling when
   he saw the snow-covered mountain.

   a   an   the

4. Dan is a _____ skier than Paul.

   fast   faster   fastest

5. Dan is the _____ downhill skier I know.

   confident   confidentest   most confident

6. Of the three skiers, Carla is the _____.

   experienced   more experienced   most experienced

7. Junie's _____ winter sport is snowboarding.

   favorite   favoriter   favoritest

8. Junie is a _____ snowboarder than Bella.

   good   better   best

9. Junie's _____ accident ever happened last year when she
   broke her arm.

   bad   worse   worst

10. Junie thinks winter sports are _____ than summer sports.

    gooder   better   more good

72

Writers choose precise words to convey ideas and emotions.
Writers use specific nouns, adjectives, verbs and adverbs to
express action and build tension.

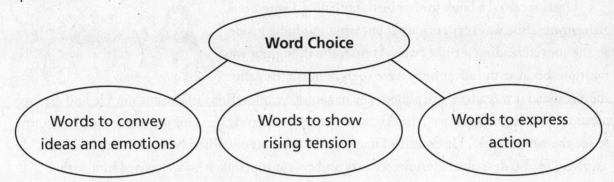

A. Read the sentences. Underline the words that convey ideas and emotions, show rising tension, and express action.

1. Wesley opened the creaky door of the crumbling cottage and peeked into the dark room.

2. A loud fluttering of wings pierced the silence.

3. Four frightened pigeons clamored their way past Wesley's face.

4. Wesley's heart pounded as he protected his face with his upraised arms.

B. Read the paragraph and underline the words that contribute to the rising tension.

   Glancing up at the clock, Melanie realized that she had only five minutes to get to the bus stop. If she missed the bus, she would be late for class—again! Miss Coleman had already warned her twice. One more time, and her grade would be lowered. Melanie grabbed her lunch, stuffed it into her backpack, and raced out the door. Immediately she realized that she had not dressed warmly enough. There was no time to go back for a jacket. She would just have to get through the day without one.

C. Think about a suspenseful experience that you have had. What vivid words could you use to convey the emotions you felt? What words could you use to build tension and express action? On a separate sheet of paper, write a short paragraph about your experience.

"Dennis the Chicken Man"
• Practice Book
© Harcourt • Grade 5

Name _____

Read the story. Circle all words with the suffix *-ous, -eous,* **or** *-ious.*

Darla received a book for her birthday called *Dangerous Adventures.* She was very curious about what might be inside, so she started reading it right away. At first, she thought it was fictitious because the adventures were so outlandish. But she soon realized it was a true story about the hazardous explorations of the author. He had explored mountainous regions, deserts, the Arctic, and tropical islands. An ambitious traveler, he wanted to see the whole world. He described many anxious moments, when he wasn't sure he would survive. He also described glorious scenery and gracious people who welcomed him with courteous gestures. The author also told of delicious foods that he had tasted on his travels. By the time she finished the book, Darla was ready to take a spontaneous trip herself, but she would have to wait until summer.

Circle and write the word that best completes each sentence.

1. Darla received a book called _____ Adventures.

   Fictitious   Ambitious   Dangerous

2. She was _____ about the book.

   anxious   furious   curious

3. Rather than being _____, it was about the true adventures of the author.

   fictitious   religious   ridiculous

4. He had gone on many _____ explorations.

   delirious   hazardous   furious

5. He had been in _____ regions, deserts, the Arctic, and tropical islands.

   mountainous   monstrous   discourteous

6. He had met many _____ people during his travels.

   discourteous   delirious   gracious

"Dennis the Chicken Man"
• **Practice Book**
© Harcourt • Grade 5

irrepressible	was	steel
feat	the	base
industry	to	bass
tendency	they	flair
device	some	dual
prestigious	put	stationary
	worker	site

1. He accomplished/ a great feat / in the industry.

2. The worker / put some glue / on the base.

3. Dr. Coover / had a flair / for inventing things.

4. He had / an irrepressible tendency / to experiment with objects.

5. The steel beams / were glued / together.

6. The material / served a dual / purpose.

7. The base / of the device / was stationary.

8. They marked / on the site / where to put glue.

9. Dr. Coover / won prestigious awards / for his invention.

10. They reattached / the peg to a bass / with that super glue.

**"Stick with Us: The Story of Harry Coover
and Super Glue" • Practice Book**
© Harcourt • Grade 5

Name _____

Read the following sentences. Underline the verb phrase.
Circle the helping verb.

1. We are feeding the ducks in the pond.

2. John was playing the guitar.

3. Jamie is writing an email to his friend.

4. Nicole and Danielle were shopping for a gift.

5. The boys have sold seven magazines for school so far.

6. My grandmother will travel to Spain this summer.

7. Becca has been working at the fair all day.

8. My sister had eaten too many chips at the party.

9. Ron is now reading the last book in the series.

10. We are cooking dinner for ten people tonight!

"Stick with Us: The Story of Harry Coover
and Super Glue" • Practice Book

Name _____

Word choice can make writing more effective. Sometimes writers have a purpose for writing that requires specific and formal words. In a letter to request something, the words a writer chooses to use are more formal than those used in a friendly letter.

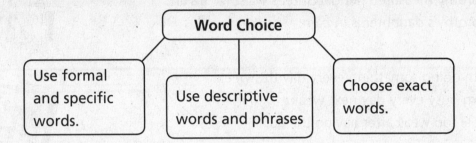

A. **Read this portion of a letter sent to a business.**

Thank you for assisting me during our phone conversation on August 10, 2006. After speaking with you, I would like to request a copy of the June 2005 edition of the Hobby Builder magazine. It would be awesome if I got it right away. I have enclosed a check for $19.95 to cover the cost of the magazine and postage. Thank you for your assistance.

B. **Use the passage to complete the directions.**

1. Circle words that give specific information.

2. Put a box around specific verbs.

3. Put a star over specific nouns related to the request.

4. Underline the sentence that needs to be rewritten using more formal and specific language. Rewrite the sentence.

_____

_____

C. **Think about a product you would like to know more about. Write a brief letter to the company that makes the product asking for more information. Use specific words and formal language to make your request.**

"Stick with Us: The Story of Harry Coover and Super Glue" • **Practice Book**
© Harcourt • Grade 5

Circle the letter in front of the sentence that best describes the picture and shows correct spelling.

1. A Dorothy does not want to waste time.

   B Dorothy measured her daughter's waist for a skirt.

   C Dorothy's daughter is in pain.

2. A I am doing something every day this week.

   B I am busy every day next weak.

   C I feel too weak after having the flu.

3. A Jeff plays the new song that he wrote on the base.

   B The base of the instrument is strong.

   C Jeff is playing the song that he wrote on the bass.

4. A They are cooking a new recipe with a steal pan.

   B Someone tried to steal my new pan.

   C The new pan on the stove is made of steel.

5. A The design of the skirt had a flare at the bottom.

   B Michael had a flair for making clothes.

   C The skirt has no flair.

6. A The stationary bike was a gift from my aunt.

   B My name is printed at the top of the stationery.

   C I am going write a letter on this stationary.

7. A This self-rising flour was used in a cake.

   B This flower is a new type of rose.

   C This flour is a new type of daisy.

"Stick with Us: The Story of Harry Coover
and Super Glue" • Practice Book
© Harcourt • Grade 5

scours	around	week
appropriate	our	spontaneous
portable	some	immature
circulate	says	mountainous
protrude		glorious
boisterous		insistent
deduction		
fickle		
practical		
measly		

1. Our teacher explained appropriate behavior / for the field trip / this week.

2. We had to be sure / our things didn't protrude / into the walkways.

3. Robin and Jessie circulate / around the room / as Andy scours the lab / for ideas.

4. In the lab, / we can turn our spontaneous ideas / into some practical inventions.

5. Andy is insistent / he will create a portable library / or book collection.

6. Robin reminds him / not to be fickle / or to act immature.

7. Jessie says / he needs just a few measly supplies / to finish his project.

8. Andy announces / in a boisterous way / that his idea will be / a success.

9. After a mountainous amount of work, / I have made / a glorious discovery myself.

10. We all agree / it is the only deduction / that can be made.

Name _____

Underline the mistakes. Write the correct pronouns on the line.

1. Please tell Sam and I what to do with ours books. _____

2. Us need to borrow his's art supplies. _____

3. Josh and him paid close attention to they're directions. _____

4. Us needed to find the materials ourself. _____

5. Rayna and her will make a moving robot. _____

6. There robot will have flashing lights on it's head. _____

7. Themselves will need to be done by this afternoon. _____

8. Mr. Thompson said, "Give youselfs a round of applause for you're fine work."

   _____

9. Sarah and me will finish ours projects early. _____

10. We gave usselfs a pat on the back. _____

Name _____

Read each sentence. Circle the mistake. Write it correctly.

1. Tie the most short ribbon in the box around this package.

   _____

2. This new joke is gooder than the other one. _____

3. This is the bestest beautiful painting I've ever seen. _____

4. The common crow is intelligenter than many birds. _____

5. I got a badder score on this test than the last one. _____

6. Tonight's sunset was the more lovely I've ever seen. _____

Read each sentence. Circle the mistakes. Write them correctly.

7. Todd can throwing an ball past the fence. _____

8. Don and Sarah am waiting for bus. _____

9. It could rained later today. _____

10. Toby will finish not his project in time. _____

11. He were running behind a others. _____

12. Later, I was eating a orange. _____

"Design Lab Field Trip" • **Practice Book**
© Harcourt • Grade 5

Read the story. Circle the Spelling Words from this lesson.

Since she was a child, Debra has wanted to be a musician. Her grandfather was a famous cellist and her mother still plays a violin. But while Debra was an applicant for a well-known music college, she discovered she had a talent for inventing. Debra's first invention was a device that could mimic the sounds of instruments. A technician could use this device to mix the sound of various instruments together into one glorious melody. This same device could also play the sound of one instrument in a melody independent from the others. This dual function made the device irreplaceable. Debra's work makes her a pioneer in music technology.

Circle and write the word that best completes each sentence.

1. Debra always wanted to be a _____.

   technician   applicant   musician

2. She is the granddaughter of a famous _____.

   violinist   cellist   breakfast

3. A _____ can use the device to blend musical sounds together.

   applicant   cellist   technician

4. The device can also make one sound _____ from another.

   independent   indefinite   insistent

5. The functions of Debra's device make it _____.

   irresponsible   irreplaceable   independent

6. Now Debra is considered a music _____.

   cellist   pioneer   engineer

basking	something	indecisive
sleek	are	invertebrate
vital	was	inorganic
damage	were	inhumane
analyzing	said	outspoken
detect	everyone	downtown
	to	uphold

1. Everyone promised / to uphold the rules / of the study.

2. In the study, / people are analyzing / the habits of frogs / and other invertebrates.

3. At the ponds, / we will detect / any inorganic matter / that does not belong.

4. The presenter said / that it is inhumane / to damage the animals' habitats.

5. On the first day, / we saw a sleek frog / basking in the sun.

6. Something was not right; / trash was everywhere.

7. A clean pond is vital / for the frog / to remain healthy.

8. We were indecisive / about what to do next.

9. We went downtown / to talk to the mayor.

10. We were outspoken / about the trash / harming the frogs.

Read the sentences below. Underline the action verbs. Circle the linking verbs.

1. Celine jogs every day.

2. The dog looked tired this morning.

3. I am happy for my brother.

4. Rob draws great cartoons.

5. The horses gallop across the field.

6. They are quiet in the library.

7. Writing is my favorite subject.

8. Aris grows flowers in her backyard.

9. I walk to the bus each day.

10. I carried Mrs. Smith's bags for her.

Effective writers use different sentence types and lengths. Combining sentences is one way to create more variety. When writing, look for short, choppy sentences that may be combined to make your writing more interesting.

| Read what you have written. | → | Look for short, choppy sentences. | → | Combine two sentences into a longer sentence. |

A. Write a new sentence that combines each pair of sentences.

1. The meeting was about a new shopping mall. It would be built on Jameson Marsh.

_____

_____

2. The wood frog population is getting smaller. This mall would destroy their habitat.

_____

_____

B. Read the paragraph. Underline the sentences that could be combined to make a longer sentence.

    The group discussed the issue. They decided to do a study. The study would look at the animal populations that live in Jameson Marsh and would analyze what would happen if the shopping mall were built on the property.

C. How do you feel about frogs? Write a short paragraph on another sheet of paper. Use a variety of sentences. Use some sentences that are combined and some that are not.

Name _____

Read the story. Circle all words with the word parts *in-*, *out-*, *down-*, and *up-*.

A hurricane was coming towards New Orleans. The aquarium in downtown New Orleans had survived other storms. Still, the keepers wanted to keep the animals safe. It was not a time to be indecisive. The keepers tried to outwit the storm. The animals from the aquarium were sent many places. Some dolphins were even placed inside hotel pools. Still, they were not able to move all of the dolphins.

When the hurricane hit, the upsurge of water broke the dolphin tank. The dolphins were swept away into the gulf. The keepers were downhearted. But before the storm, the keepers had placed locators on the dolphins. They would use these to find the dolphins.

A number of people began looking. The outreach of people wanting to help was incredible. All eight dolphins were found together. The keepers' spirits were uplifted by the news. Some of the dolphins were sick, but the keepers remained upbeat. The dolphins had survived the hurricane.

Circle and write the word that best completes each sentence.

1. The aquarium was located in _____ New Orleans.

   downplay   indecisive   downtown

2. When a hurricane is on its way, it is not the time to be _____.

   indecisive   outpatient   uptight

3. The keepers were _____ when the dolphins were swept into the gulf.

   downplayed   downhearted   uplifted

4. The number of people wanting to search for the dolphins was _____.

   inconsiderate   outranked   incredible

5. The keepers' spirits were _____ when they found all of the dolphins.

   incompetent   uplifted   indecisive

6. Even though the dolphins were sick, the keepers remained _____.

   upbeat   downbeat   outwitted

somberly	the	organization
stammers	to	passion
monopolize	you	repetition
deflated	are	champion
enraptured	was	confusion
enterprising	what	dedication
cumbersome	have	

1. We looked somberly / at the park.

2. We started / the cumbersome job / of picking it up.

3. "What if we ask / the city to help?" / asked Sarika.

4. Celine was stammering / while watching the confusion / at the meeting.

5. The adults / monopolized most / of the meeting.

6. They said / we could form / an organization.

7. We were deflated / that there was / no money available.

8. Our passion / for the project / kept us going.

9. The repetition of cleaning was tiring, / but we are enraptured / with a clean park.

10. We will have a dedication / to celebrate / our clean park.

Name _____

Circle the correct word. Write it on the blank.

1. The bat _____ the peach.

   eat   eats   eates

2. The cars _____ down the race track.

   speeds   speed   speedes

3. Bill _____ his little brother.

   watch   watchs   watches

4. The bee _____ loudly on the window.

   buzz   buzzs   buzzes

5. Katie _____ the magazines on the counter.

   sets   sit   sits

6. We watch as the sun _____ over the trees.

   rise   rises   raises

7. My brother _____ to tie his shoes.

   try   trys   tries

8. Hannah and Garrett _____ to play tennis.

   like   likes   likies

9. Dad _____ our car every Saturday.

   wash   washs   washes

10. Mom _____ when I am late.

    worry   worrys   worries

"Elm Street Speaks!" • Practice Book

© Harcourt • Grade 5

When writing a persuasive paragraph you should use effective sentences. **Effective sentences** give reasons, details, and examples. When you voice an opinion, first think of the reason for your opinion. Then think of details and examples to support your reasons.

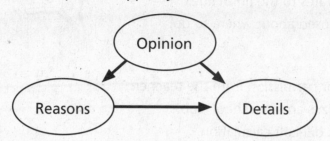

A. Read the sentences below. Put a box around the opinion. Draw a circle around the reason. Underline the details.

We should not lengthen the school day. It would mean that students would have less time for extracurricular activities. There would not be enough time after school for baseball and soccer practice. Our baseball and soccer fields do not have lights, so we cannot practice at night.

B. Read the paragraph below. Identify the author's opinion, reason, and details.

People talk a lot about what teachers can do to make the school a better place. I think that the students can make a bigger difference. There are more students than teachers, so we could have more impact. Perhaps one group of students could clean up the outside. Another group might decide to start a tutoring club afterschool. Another group could have a book drive for the library. The possibilities are unlimited. If each student chose one project to make our school better, imagine how great our school could be.

Opinion: _____

Reason 1: _____

Detail 1: _____

Detail 2: _____

Detail 3: _____

C. Copy the chart above onto a separate sheet of paper. Imagine you are writing a paragraph to your school newsletter supporting or opposing school uniforms. Use the chart to plan your article.

"Elm Street Speaks!" • Practice Book
© Harcourt • Grade 5

Name _____

Circle the letter in front of the sentence that best describes the picture.

1. **A** Clarice is the champion of the track meet.
   B Clarice accelerates to the finish line.
   C Clarice is confused about where to go.

2. **A** Miguel asks for permission from the teacher.
   B Miguel organizes an afterschool club.
   C Miguel does a difficult calculation.

3. **A** The car accelerates to pass the truck.
   B The car arrives at the mansion.
   C The car is in front of the apartment in the city.

4. **A** The snow plow removed the snow from the street.
   B The snow made a large hill for sledding.
   C There is a large accumulation of snow.

5. **A** Be careful around the demolition site!
   B The house is being repainted before it is sold.
   C The wind broke several of the windows.

6. **A** Tawna was careful to avoid the muddy puddle.
   B Tawna was glad to have a companion for the walk.
   C Tawna tripped clumsily, dropping her backpack.

7. **A** Everyone could see the tension on the rope.
   B The rope broke causing one team to fall.
   C The children cheered when one team moved across the line.

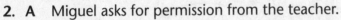
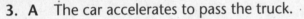
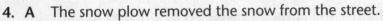
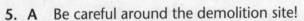
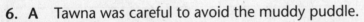

gouges	they	delight
desolate	the	autumn
bustles	was	hasten
fervor	shoes	scenery
immaculate	could	knowledge
assuage	one	debris
		assign
		solemn

1. April's new puppy, / Buttons, / was a delight / when she first saw him.

2. She could just imagine / taking him for walks / in the autumn.

3. They would hasten / down the sidewalk, / enjoying the scenery / along the way.

4. However, / April's knowledge of dogs / was limited, / and Buttons / was a handful.

5. "That dog gouges every one / of my shoes!" / April's mother complained.

6. April defended the dog / with great fervor, / not wishing to assign him / any blame.

7. To assuage her mom, / she said she'd show Buttons / the damaged shoes.

8. A desolate April / looked for Buttons, / but could not find him anywhere.

9. Her neighbor, / Mrs. Ramirez, / bustles around her immaculate yard, / picking up debris.

10. "Have you seen my dog?" / April asked Mrs. Ramirez / in a solemn voice.

Name _____

Write the correct simple present, simple past, or simple future
tense of the verb shown in parentheses.

1. Last year, Jack _____ on the local baseball team. (play)

2. Jack _____ out for football last week. (try)

3. Tomorrow, Jack _____ for two hours. (practice)

4. Yesterday, Margie _____ on a bus at three o'clock. (hop)

5. Jack _____ every day before practice. (stretch)

6. Margie _____ a train to visit her sister next week. (take)

7. In about a month, Margie _____ her mom's birthday party. (attend)

8. On Mondays, Margie _____ Mrs. Harper's toddler. (watch)

9. Jack and Margie _____ to some old music at last night's party. (dance)

10. Yesterday, Jack _____ for a new shirt. (look)

11. Do you think they _____ for shoes tomorrow? (shop)

12. Their mother already _____ them find new shoes. (help)

13. Now April _____ her dog around the block. (walk)

14. On weekends, she _____ a dog training class. (attend)

"The Quiet Neighbor" • Practice Book

To persuade readers, you must clearly state your opinion. Then you must develop your arguments with specific details and examples. Use colorful examples and effective images to develop your ideas.

A. Identify the persuasive elements in this poem.

I scowled at my pup

as he grasped my pants leg.

"This pup must be hungry!"

I said as he begged.

Though I gave him a treat,

With a roll of his eyes,

He seemed to be asking,

"Can't you just read my mind?"

But I haven't a clue

As to what my dog needs;

I'm not very good at this sort of thing.

So the next time you decide to get a new pet,

Be sure and pick up some tips from a vet!

1. Underline the part that tells you the author's opinion.

2. Circle the detail that tells you that the author is guessing what the pup needs.

3. Put a box around the detail that tells you that the author doesn't know how to care for a puppy.

B. Read the passage. Then underline the parts that give the writer's opinion.

Good manners are important in dogs, that's for sure.

They must not beg for food. They should not pull on

leashes or jump on company. These actions are

sure to keep your guests away.

C. Think about an issue or idea about which you have a strong opinion. What colorful examples and specific details would help you convince others to agree with you? Write your list on a separate sheet of paper.

Name _____

Circle the letter in front of the sentence that best describes the picture.

1. **A** They knead the dough.
   B They design the wreath.
   C They whirl around.

2. **A** The boys wrestled.
   B The boys hasten home.
   C Debris clutters up the ring.

3. **A** Autumn comes early.
   B She enjoys the scenery.
   C Lightning strikes a tree.

4. **A** He does a thorough job.
   B He will soon resign from this job.
   C It is a solemn occasion.

5. **A** The shelves glisten.
   B Debris clutters the shelves.
   C She searches for knowledge.

6. **A** He will resign from his job.
   B He will assign the work.
   C He takes delight in his job.

7. **A** He finds a crumb.
   B He makes a rhyme.
   C He makes a wreath.

"The Quiet Neighbor" • **Practice Book**
© Harcourt • Grade 5

excursions	you	opportunities
giddy	said	radios
pinnacle	was	echoes
gleeful	come	knives
panic	into	addresses
turbulent	here	shelves
precious	to	

1. My shelves of model airplanes / are precious / to me.

2. I was giddy / when my uncle said / I could fly with him.

3. As a pilot, / he had opportunities / for excursions / around the world.

4. We fly / high into the sky.

5. On the radios, / we hear reports / of turbulent air.

6. I felt as if / knives were / in my stomach.

7. "You must not panic!" / his voice echoes / in the cockpit.

8. Radio addresses / tell us / to come back.

9. When he said, / "Here we are / on the ground," / I was gleeful.

10. This was the pinnacle / of my summer vacation.

Complete each sentence by writing the correct tense of the verb, as indicated after the sentence.

1. They _____ thirty books by the end of the year.
   (*read*, future perfect)

2. They _____ helping with safety patrol.
   (*be*, present perfect)

3. They _____ to be library helpers in March.
   (*want*, past perfect)

4. She _____ her goldfish too much food.
   (*feed*, present perfect)

5. Miguel _____ the pizza by now.
   (*order*, future perfect)

6. If this downpour keeps up, it _____ several inches by morning. (*rain*, future perfect)

7. Katrina _____ three science awards.
   (*win*, past perfect)

8. Mr. Smith and Mrs. Lopez _____ for ten years.
   (*teach*, present perfect)

9. No one _____ that many laps before.
   (*jog*, past perfect)

10. By noon, we _____ a thousand cans for the Food Drive. (*pack*, future perfect)

"Carmine's Backyard" • Practice Book
© Harcourt • Grade 5

Name _____

A fictional story includes a setting, characters, and plot events.
The use of figurative language can develop supporting details about
these story elements. Supporting details develop the story and move
the plot along. Ideas should be organized so the story unfolds logically.

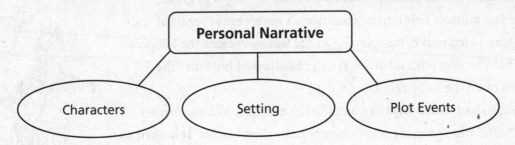

A. Read the paragraph. Underline the words that describe the setting. Circle the characters' names.

Radar flew into the cold, black cave. It was dark, but bats like it that way. He was on the lookout for Blackie. Blackie had taken a piece of peach right out of his mouth.

B. Read the sentences. Underline the figurative language used to provide supporting details.

The shot of the starter's gun rang in his ears. Jason thought of himself, a torpedo, moving through the air. He leapt across the starting line with all of his strength. He pushed forward until he felt as if his lungs would burst like a balloon.

C. Now it's your turn to think about the development of a story. On a separate sheet of paper, write the beginning of a story about losing a pet. Introduce the characters, the setting, and the plot by using details and figurative language. Hint at how the conflict might be resolved.

"Carmine's Backyard" • Practice Book
© Harcourt • Grade 5

Name _____

Read the story. Circle all the plural words.

Decoding/Spelling:
Unusual Plurals
. . . .
Lesson 24

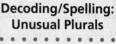

Our class field trip to the zoo was a great learning experience. It started out badly, though. Our buses were late. Then the teacher forgot to add the taxes to our ticket prices. After that, the trip was great.

We saw animals from many countries. There were several babies. We saw some elephant calves playing in the water. We saw the keepers feeding baby wolves with a bottle. We were surprised how tiny the hooves were on the baby zebras.

We also had some surprises outside the exhibits. We saw armies of ants. Some were carrying leaves bigger than their bodies. It looked as if they were making tiny volcanoes in the sand. As we were leaving, we could hear the echoes of the monkeys chattering. It was definitely our favorite trip. We were so glad that our teacher made copies of her video.

Circle and write the word that best completes each sentence.

1. The students had many _____ to learn at the zoo.

   opportunities   books   wishes

2. The elephant _____ raised their trunks to the students.

   litters   calves   keepers

3. There were animals from many _____.

   countries   worlds   continents

4. The school _____ arrived at the zoo late.

   trips   letters   buses

5. The teacher made extra _____ of the zoo trip.

   photos   videos   pictures

6. The _____ were being fed by the keepers.

   lions   monkeys   wolves

"Carmine's Backyard" • Practice Book
© Harcourt • Grade 5

loathe	friend	indecisive
bland	they	wrestled
dilapidated	doing	radios
coordination	the	knowledge
sensibility	are	champion
compassionate		
advocacy		
mistreated		
mentor		
altruism		

1. A group of / compassionate kids / was committed to advocacy.

2. They were indecisive / and wrestled / with how to start.

3. With some knowledge and compassion, / they were able / to champion several causes.

4. One friend / with artistic sensibility / painted dilapidated houses.

5. These bland homes / are now beautiful.

6. They were loathe / to leave animals / out of their work.

7. Another student found homes / for mistreated pets.

8. Their mentor helped them / get radios / for emergency kits.

9. They were all / doing what they could / to get the word out.

10. All of the students were proud / of their altruism / and their efforts!

Name _____

Underline the verbs. Write *action* or *linking* to identify each.

1. Allie reads three books each week. _____

2. John feels tired after the race. _____

3. Lila is our student council member. _____

4. Jamal plays chess at the park. _____

5. The girls tutor a group of little kids. _____

Rewrite the sentences with the correct subject/verb agreement.

6. Josh wish for a new video game.

   _____

7. You gives great gifts.

   _____

8. Maya hurry down the hall.

   _____

9. We wants to go fishing.

   _____

10. Lila and Maya is two girls in my class.

   _____

11. The two dogs and I was running across the field.

   _____

"Kid Power!" • Practice Book

Name _____

Identify and circle the correct tense of each underlined verb.

1. The boys <u>will practice</u> tomorrow.

   past tense   present tense   future tense

2. I <u>saw</u> Mrs. Smith yesterday.

   past tense   present tense   future tense

3. Lauren <u>will have</u> Mr. Juarez next year.

   past perfect tense   present perfect tense   future tense

4. We <u>had visited</u> the museum last year.

   past perfect tense   present perfect tense   future perfect tense

5. Tara <u>gets</u> off the bus.

   past tense   present tense   future tense

6. She <u>has jumped</u> off the diving board.

   past perfect tense   present perfect tense   future perfect tense

7. I <u>looked</u> over the paper before I turned it in.

   past tense   present tense   future tense

Name _____

Read the story. Then circle the letter of the answer that makes each sentence below tell about the story.

Max looked out at the rainy, wet day. He was indecisive about what to do at first. The streets were wet from the rain. With a sigh, he got his running shoes and rain jacket off the shelves. He grabbed one of his radios.

He had wrestled with going out in the rain, but now that he saw the scenery, he was glad he had gone. He loved the colorful autumn leaves everywhere. Some were as red as tomatoes, and others were a beautiful golden color. It was like running on a colorful carpet. "Enough of enjoying the scenery," he murmured. "If I am going to be a marathon champion, I need to get going." He thought of the beginning of the race where everyone was lined up like armies ready to attack. He picked up his pace, feeling the acceleration in every muscle.

Last year, he had barely finished. This year, he had more knowledge and experience. As Max rounded the last corner, he imagined his house was the finish line, cameras everywhere. He could see his image on the videos as he received his trophy. Only three more days, he thought with a smile.

1. Why had Max wrestled with running?
   A He had overslept.
   B He had not eaten breakfast.
   C It was raining outside.
   D He didn't have rain gear.

2. Why were the leaves on the ground?
   A Tornadoes blew them down.
   B It was autumn.
   C Armies were trimming the trees.
   D Max knocked them down.

3. Why is Max running?
   A He was making videos.
   B He doesn't want to get wet.
   C He is indecisive.
   D He wants to be marathon champion.

4. How does Max describe the beginning of the race?
   A Everyone is lined up like armies.
   B There is a lack of acceleration.
   C The drink stations are everywhere.
   D There is beautiful scenery.

5. How did Max do in the marathon last year?
   A He was the race champion.
   B He barely finished the race.
   C He wrestled with the pace.
   D He was uptight and didn't finish.

6. How is Max feeling about the race?
   A He needs his parents' authorization.
   B He is indecisive.
   C He feels he needs more knowledge.
   D He feels he can be a champion.

Name _____

asset	were	unsuccessful
profusely	again	immeasurable
terrain	airplane	disloyalty
peril	many	replacement
intently	something	impossibly
ordeal		encouragement
dismal		reassurance
esteem		

1. A team of scientists / who were held in high esteem / wanted to build a new aircraft.

2. Their idea / was to invent something different / that would be an asset / to their country.

3. Although the group / had immeasurable talent, / their efforts were unsuccessful.

4. Many an ordeal / made the work feel / impossibly long and dismal.

5. Still, / the team worked intently / on their project / with no disloyalty among them.

6. They gave each other reassurance / and encouragement / even in difficult times.

7. It was raining profusely / when they finally planned / to test their aircraft.

8. The weather and difficult terrain / put their test / in peril.

9. The airplane flew well, / but a wheel and wing were damaged / when it landed.

10. The team decided / to find replacement parts / and try their test again.

"Charles Lindbergh, the Lone Eagle"
• Practice Book
© Harcourt • Grade 5

Name _____

Read each sentence. Underline the verb or verb phrase. Circle the helping verbs. Then identify the verb form in the sentence by writing *present*, *present participle*, *past*, or *past participle* on the line.

1. Kim and Li play soccer.

   _____

2. Their team won the championship game in their state.

   _____

3. They are flying to California for the national championship.

   _____

4. Both girls have flown many times before.

   _____

5. Each likes to sit by the window.

   _____

6. Their parents have begun to pack for the big trip.

   _____

7. The girls are excited about the whole adventure.

   _____

8. Their coach has seen the game on television before.

   _____

9. She knows what an exciting event it will be.

   _____

10. Everyone in town has heard about the big game.

   _____

A paragraph that explains tells how or why something happens or happened. All the ideas in the paragraph are focused on one main topic.

> A topic sentence states the main idea in the paragraph.

> Important details and examples focus on the main idea. Extra or repeated information is left out.

> The topic tells why or how something happens or happened.

A. Read each topic sentence. Then circle the letter of the idea that focuses on the topic.

1. **Topic sentence:** A pilot must be well trained.
   A   Pilots often are gone for several days at a time.
   B   A pilot must have many hours of flight instruction.

2. **Topic sentence:** An airplane has equipment that helps a pilot navigate in bad weather.
   A   One device tells the pilot how high the airplane is flying.
   B   Some airplanes have telephones built into the passenger seats.

3. **Topic sentence:** The design of airplanes has changed greatly over time.
   A   In large airplanes, propellers have been replaced with jet engines.
   B   The price of a ticket is less expensive now than it was in the past.

B. Read the passage below. Then circle the sentence that shares the same focus.

Controllers stay in contact with pilots during the flight. When they reach their destination, the pilots listen for the air traffic controllers to give directions about where and when to land.

1. The controllers must also think about how the weather will affect the airplane.

2. The runways at an airport are lit for planes landing after dark.

3. Not everyone likes to fly in an airplane.

C. On a separate sheet of paper, write two possible topic sentences for the paragraph above.

"Charles Lindbergh, the Lone Eagle"
• Practice Book
© Harcourt • Grade 5

Name _____

Read the story. Circle all words with a prefix + root + suffix.

"Will you build a paper airplane for me?" asked Maria.

"Yes, Maria," Roberto said with reassurance. He was undoubtedly the best airplane builder in the family.

"I want you to make one that is unbreakable!" shouted Maria as she jumped unsafely on the couch.

"I'm not sure such an airplane can be made," laughed Roberto.

"I know you can do it. You are the best builder in the world," said an impossibly loud Maria.

"Thanks for the encouragement," said Roberto as he folded the last wing and unselfishly handed the airplane to his sister.

"Unbelievable! This is the best!" she cried as she ran from the room.

Minutes later, Maria returned with the crumpled airplane. Immeasurable damage had been done. She looked at Roberto with tears in her eyes and asked, "Can I have a replacement?"

Roberto smiled and handed her a new plane. "I thought you might need one," he grinned.

Circle and write the word that best completes each sentence.

1. Maria wanted an airplane that was _____.

   unbelievable   unbreakable   undoubtedly

2. Roberto answered her with _____.

   reassurance   reaction   renewal

3. Maria was _____ loud when she spoke to her brother.

   immeasurable   impassable   impossibly

4. Maria jumped _____ on the couch.

   unsafely   unlikable   unselfishly

5. Maria did _____ damage to the airplane.

   unbreakable   immeasurable   impassible

6. Roberto had a _____ airplane ready for Maria.

   rearrangement   reappearance   replacement

"Charles Lindbergh, the Lone Eagle"
• Practice Book

remote	friends	disaster
laden	their	chronicle
appalled	they'd	chronic
invest	become	chronology
floundered	anyone	synchronize
grueling	was	hydrate
isolated		optical

1. The explorers traveled / to a remote location / in their dog sleds.

2. They'd been moving / at a grueling pace / for what seemed like days.

3. The driver of the sled / knew it would be a disaster / if they didn't rest and hydrate.

4. Being tired and thirsty / might cause chronic headaches / and optical illusions.

5. Laden with supplies, / they found an isolated cave / to rest in and synchronize plans.

6. The team / had become close friends / on this journey.

7. Each was appalled / to think that / they might not finish the trip together.

8. Their conversations / were mostly about the trip / and the chronology of events.

9. They had floundered / once or twice / but did not give up.

10. They wanted to chronicle the trip / and share it with anyone / who would invest a moment / to listen.

"To the Arctic with Matthew Henson"
• Practice Book
© Harcourt • Grade 5

Circle the correct word to complete each sentence. Write the word in the blank.

1. _____ not easy to live in a very cold climate.

    Its   It's

2. _____ time is spent working to keep the machines running well.

    Your   You're

3. People have to be prepared so that _____ animals are warm and fed.

    they're   their

4. Deciding _____ responsibility it is to care for the animals is important.

    whose   who's

5. I _____ want to be caught without supplies during the winter.

    isn't   wouldn't

6. _____ never sure when the next big snow will come.

    Your   You're

7. I can tell my dog senses a storm when it puts _____ nose in the air and sniffs.

    it's   its

8. Sometimes we wonder _____ going to plow the snow from our road.

    who's   whose

9. My parents know that it is not easy to get _____ car out after a storm.

    your   you're

10. We _____ have warm enough coats for the weather.

    doesn't   didn't

"To the Arctic with Matthew Henson"
• **Practice Book**
© Harcourt • Grade 5

Most paragraphs begin with a main idea or focus statement.
The other sentences that follow support the main idea.

All sentences in the paragraph support the topic.	→ ←	Paragraph is focused on a single topic.	→ ←	Details and examples explain the topic.

A. Read each pair of sentences. Write T next to the one that would make a better topic. Write D next to the detail sentence that supports the topic.

Example Traveling in a cold climate takes special preparation. ___**T**___

You should always wear boots and gloves. ___**D**___

1. One winter Sam skied every day. _____

   Sam loves outdoor activities in the winter. _____

2. Traveling with a group can help you stay safe. _____

   People look out for each other. _____

3. You can find out the best places to eat and rest. _____

   You can benefit by learning from the local people. _____

B. Read the paragraph below. Underline the topic sentence. Then circle the phrases that contain supporting details.

   The Arctic region is a beautiful and dangerous place. How can this be? Miles of perfectly white snow and ice cover the land. Without trees, plants, or other barriers, the wind can be fierce. The blowing snow and ice often cause explorers to lose track of their direction.

C. Tell about a place you have visited. Write a focused topic sentence and at least two details that support it. Use another sheet of paper.

Read the story. Then circle the letter of the answer that makes each sentence below tell about the story.

Ellen always dreamed of being an astronaut. Her favorite subject in school was astronomy. She had memorized the sections about space in all the encyclopedias that her family owned. She could not imagine any other job. That is why when disaster almost ruined her dreams, Ellen fought back.

The exact chronology of events is hard to track because things happened very quickly. One day, Ellen was riding her bicycle and enjoying the warm summer sun, and the next day, she was unable to focus her blurred vision. After several visits to her optician, Ellen learned that she suffered from a chronic dry eye condition. She would need to hydrate her eyes with drops regularly and hope for the best.

Luckily, because she caught the problem early, the treatment was a success. Ellen grew up to fulfill her dreams of becoming an astronaut and studied the path of asteroids around Earth.

1. What was Ellen's dream as a child?
   A to be an optician
   B to ride on an asteroid
   C to become an astronaut
   D to write a book

2. What kind of books did Ellen read and memorize?
   A history books
   B astronomy picture books
   C encyclopedias
   D comic books

3. What was the symptom of Ellen's eye problem?
   A blurred vision
   B blindness
   C tearing
   D itching eyes

4. What kind of doctor did Ellen visit?
   A pediatrician
   B optician
   C dentist
   D dermatologist

5. What treatment did Ellen follow?
   A She wore an eye patch.
   B She did not go into the sun.
   C She wore dark glasses.
   D She hydrated her eyes with drops.

6. What does Ellen study in her job?
   A the life of astronauts
   B the path of the sun
   C the path of asteroids around Earth
   D eye conditions and treatments

"To the Arctic with Matthew Henson"
• Practice Book
© Harcourt • Grade 5

Name _____

summit	was	traction
accustomed	have	contract
secure	everything	interrupt
essential	anywhere	auditorium
streamlined	done	dictate
acclimate	their	predict
	to	
	together	

1. The students got together / in the auditorium / for an assembly.

2. Their science teacher / wanted to acclimate them / to a new streamlined class project.

3. The plan was / to interrupt regular classes / and visit the summit / of the mountain.

4. The students were not accustomed / to going anywhere / so exciting.

5. Everyone needed / to sign a contract / that would dictate the rules / for the trip.

6. It was essential / that they have everything done / before they were allowed / to go.

7. The trip was at night / so the students could view / the constellations.

8. It was hard to predict / what they would see.

9. The teacher made sure / they understood / how to secure their safety equipment.

10. Everyone needed hiking boots / to be sure they had good traction / for climbing.

"Life in Space" • Practice Book
© Harcourt • Grade 5

Complete each sentence by circling the correct form of the
adverb. Write your answer in the blank.

1. Pat ran _____ than Mike.

   fast   faster   fastest

2. Mike tried the _____ of all the children on the team.

   hard   harder   hardest

3. He learned the games _____.

   quickly   quick   more quick

4. He and his friends did _____ give up.

   never   not never   not

5. They played _____ than their competition.

   skillfully   skillfuller   more skillfully

6. The players practiced _____ than last year.

   more regularly   most regularly   regularly

7. Mike arrived _____ to the game.

   early   earliest   earlier

8. He _____ prepared the equipment for the game.

   more busily   most busily   busily

9. The game was the _____ played of the season.

   most intensely   intensely   more intensely

10. Their victory won't _____ be forgotten.

    never   ever   neither

Name _____

When writing a how-to paragraph, it is important to use correct writing **conventions**, such as capitalization, punctuation, grammar, and spelling. This will make your writing more clear and help the reader to understand what you are trying to say.

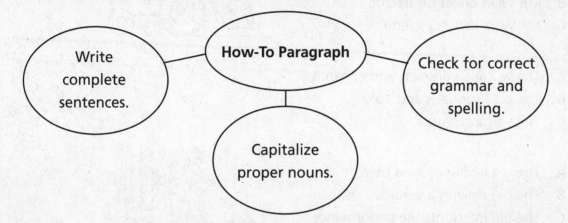

A. **Read the sentences. Find the errors in capitalization, grammar, punctuation, and spelling. Then rewrite each sentence correctly.**

1. Marissa and kate loved to look at the stars? _____

_____

2. The girls, often go on hikes at night _____

_____

3. A Shooting Star streaked across the nite sky. _____

_____

B. **Read the paragraph. Circle the errors in capitalization, punctuation, grammar, and spelling.**

an Eclipse is a rare event. There are eclipses of the sun and the moon? You can only view an eclipse, of the sun, by looking through a specal device. Otherwise, The power of the sun could Damage a person's eyes. An eclipse of the moon is safer to view.

C. **Rewrite the paragraph above on another sheet of paper. Be sure to make all the corrections in capitalization, punctuation, grammar, and spelling. Then give the paragraph a title.**

"Life in Space" • **Practice Book**
© Harcourt • Grade 5

Circle the letter in front of the sentence that best describes the picture.

1. **A** Mr. Wells auditions for a play.
    B Mr. Wells drives his tractor.
    C Mr. Wells dictates a letter.

2. **A** The volcano contracts and expands.
    B The pipe ruptures and leaks.
    C The volcano erupts.

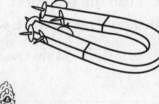

3. **A** The girl auditions for a play.
    B The girl delivers a verdict.
    C The girl interrupts the performance.

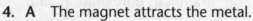

4. **A** The magnet attracts the metal.
    B The magnet interrupts the metal.
    C The magnet causes the metal to contract.

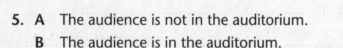

5. **A** The audience is not in the auditorium.
    B The audience is in the auditorium.
    C The audience is on the stage.

6. **A** Sarah read the verdict.
    B Sarah read a prediction.
    C Sarah read a dictionary.

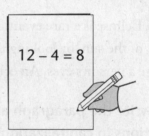

7. **A** You need to subtract to solve this problem.
    B This answer is an incorrect prediction.
    C The answer to this problem was dictated incorrectly.

$$12 - 4 = 8$$

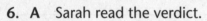

"Life in Space" • Practice Book
© Harcourt • Grade 5

Name _____

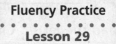
ignited	beautiful	cousin
potentially	to	stomach
squinting	what	yogurt
tranquility	there	chocolate
cramped	into	vanilla
jettisoned	have	banana
	was	anchor

1. Last year, / I went on an adventure / with my cousin.

2. We sailed / on a large boat / to a beautiful island.

3. When we were close to the island, / we were jettisoned into a cove.

4. The tiny craft was small and cramped, / but the tranquility of the water / was amazing.

5. The crew dropped an anchor / near the shore, / and my stomach jumped.

6. The island was yards away, / and we would have to swim / to get there.

7. Squinting to see, / I thought it seemed / potentially difficult to reach.

8. Then my cousin reminded me / that once there, / we would get frozen yogurt.

9. I am not sure what got into me, / but my energy ignited, / and I jumped right in.

10. The chocolate, / vanilla, / and banana treat / was the perfect reward / after the long swim.

115

Read the letter. Circle the mistakes. Then rewrite the letter correctly.

november 21 2008

Dear Uncle Ted

it was nice to visit with you last weekend. I hope that we can go camping again soon did you catch any fish after I left?

Your nephew Matt

_____

_____

_____

_____

_____

Read the excerpt from a story below. Circle the mistakes. Then rewrite the passage correctly on another sheet of paper.

This is the best book of the year, said Tom.

Sam said, "did you tell Mr. Watson about it?"

"Yes. I wrote him a letter. Here is what it said," explained Tom.

December 30, 2008

Dear Mr. Watson

I wanted to tell you about a new book that I read. The title is journey to the islands. Many people say that it is the best book in years. I agree. Matthew smith from kansas city wrote an article about it in the newspaper.

I hope you will take the time to read this book, too. You will not be disappointed.

sincerely

Tom johnson

Name _____

Using correct capitalization and punctuation **conventions** in your writing will help others understand what you are trying to say.

Writing Trait:
Conventions
• • • • • • • •
Lesson 29

```
                    ┌─────────────────┐
                    │   Conventions   │
                    └─────────────────┘
```

| Use correct capitalization and punctuation in sentences. | Punctuate titles and quotations correctly. | Sentences are complete and grammar is correct. | Words are spelled correctly. |

A. Read the passage below.

galileo was an Italian scientist. He studied many things and he was greatly interested in the stars and night sky which he liked to spend time observing. Special lenses that were invented in holland helped him to build his own telescope? He used this telescope to discover craters on the Moon, sunspots, the four largest satellites of jupiter, and the phases of the planet Venus. Galileo published his findings in a book called The starry Messenger.

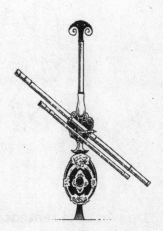

B. Use the passage to answer the questions.

Example   Write the word from the first sentence that should be capitalized.

Galileo

1. Circle the sentence that is a run-on.

2. Which proper nouns in this passage should be capitalized but are not?

_____

3. Underline the sentence that has the wrong end punctuation.

4. Write the title of Galileo's book correctly.

_____

C. Now rewrite the passage on another sheet of paper, correcting the mistakes in capitalization and punctuation.

"To the South Pacific"
• **Practice Book**
© Harcourt • Grade 5

117

Do what the sentences tell you to do.

1. Tia and Ramona are cousins. They look alike. Color their hair the same color.

2. They also like to dress alike. Draw a red triangle on their shirts over their stomachs.

3. The girls like to ride in their friend's kayak. Draw a kayak on the water and color it green.

4. Tia's favorite animal is a chimpanzee. Color the chimpanzee in the tree brown.

5. The chimpanzee has picked a banana. Draw a banana in the chimp's hand.

6. There is a boathouse on the beach. Draw an anchor on the door.

7. Ramona's family owns the boathouse. They call it LOSA. It is an acronym that means "Love Our Seas Always." Write this acronym above the door.

8. Find the replica of a ship. Circle it.

9. Tia brought along her parka and left it on the beach. Find the parka and color it orange.

10. Ramona left her backpack on the ground. Draw an almanac next to her backpack.

poised	wherever	cousin
earnestly	what's	urban
insufficient	aren't	immeasurable
exceptional	you	contract
achievement	once	language
bickering		
equivalent		
regal		
customary		
provoke		

1. Once., my cousin and I / decided to visit / a national forest.

2. We are from an urban area, / so there was an immeasurable difference / in this place.

3. Wherever we go, / there's usually a lot of bickering / between us.

4. This time, / I earnestly tried not to provoke / any disagreements.

5. Once in the forest, / we realized / we'd packed an insufficient amount / of supplies.

6. Our guide said, / "It is customary / for you to bring the equivalent / of two days' food."

7. I realized / that I must not have read the language / in the contract completely.

8. I was poised / for an argument / when my cousin started to speak.

9. "What's the problem? / Aren't we brave explorers?" / she asked in a regal voice.

10. Our trip turned out / to be an exceptional achievement / because we didn't fight once.

Name _____

Underline the irregular verb or the contraction. Write them correctly on the line.

1. We begun our hike when the guide gave us directions. _____

2. He told us we should'nt become separated from the group. _____

3. My friends and I singed songs to make the walk more fun. _____

4. Ih've been to this part of the nature park before. _____

5. My sister decided that she wouldnt come again. _____

6. She haved a bad experience here last month. _____

7. She tripped over a log and felled on the ground. _____

8. She w'snot hurt, but she decided not to hike anymore this year. _____

9. I weared my new hiking boots. _____

10. Hopefully theyw'll keep me from tripping as I walk. _____

"Exploring Caves" • Practice Book

Look for mistakes in adverb use and punctuation. Then write the sentence correctly.

1. "The movie was wonderful said mary

   _____

2. It was called fast train home.

   _____

3. We hadn't never seen a movie like it before.

   _____

4. Will you come to see it with me? asked Mark.

   _____

5. Mark listened careful to a new song called the mailbox blues.

   _____

6. Have you read the poem called Paper Dreams?" asked Sam?

   _____

7. I read that poem slow than my cousin did.

   _____

8. Let's get to the theater earliest than anyone else," Said Tim.

   _____

Name _____

Circle the letter in front of the sentence that best describes the picture.

1. **A** Mary could see great immeasurable light in the cave.
   B Mary thought the cave seemed impossibly dark.
   C Mary didn't think she'd need the unbreakable flashlight in the bright cave.

2. **A** Sam looked through the telescope to see the path of the asteroid.
   B Sam gave up looking for the reappearance of the object.
   C Sam broke the optical viewing lens on his telescope.

3. **A** Sarah wrote the chronology of events in her journal.
   B Sarah swam in the water with too much chlorine.
   C Sarah needed to hydrate after the long race.

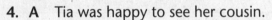

4. **A** Tia was happy to see her cousin.
   B Tia and Maria signed the contract.
   C Tia and Maria found it impossibly hard to get along.

5. **A** This book teaches about the Polish language.
   B This book is an almanac with information about the weather.
   C This book is about a cyclone that happened in 1990.

6. **A** Theresa tested the chlorine in the family pool.
   B Theresa looked at the town from the balcony.
   C Theresa talked about the weather with her cousin.

7. **A** Mrs. Brown was bankrupt.
   B Mrs. Brown read the newspaper on the balcony.
   C Mrs. Brown bought an almanac for her son.

122